# Foreword to Second Edition

*"Pilsdon is like a grain of salt: sharp and refreshing: tiny in the context of the wider world, but strangely pervasive: something simple, but for many people very precious"*

John MacAuslan, Chairman of the Trustees
(on the 40th Anniversary of the founding of the Community in 1998)

The interest on the part of many in reading the story of the beginnings of the Pilsdon Community has prompted us to reprint Gaynor Smith's unique account. We are most grateful to her for allowing us to do so.

It has been without doubt the founding vision and energy of Percy and Gaynor Smith that has given the peculiar savour to this enterprise that has lasted over the years. But it has also been sustained by the commitment and vision of those who have come after. Inevitably there have been changes and adaptations to the needs of a new generation, but no-one who experienced the early years would be in any doubt that today we are the same "Pilsdon". The faces may change but the stories are still familiar.

As in the beginning, seven or eight people have renounced a private home and ordinary family life to create a household of some forty people where all are welcome. The cows are still milked by hand and the garden worked to be productive. Those who come as strangers are honoured as guests: they are valued not for what they do, or earn, or own or achieve. Many will bring with them crisis or anguish. Accepting people with their pain without attempting to fit them within a professional therapeutic structure inevitably makes the community vulnerable, but can sometimes give healing beyond the reach of professional care alone.

Nothing is imposed on guests by way of religious activity; but Pilsdon's soul is Christian: with the church in the garden and the daily round of prayer in the household chapel, it is for many people a holy place; a place where prayer has been valid, with a continuity stretching back not just over 40 years but to the Little Gidding community of 350 years ago and the monastic communities of earlier centuries.

Whether you are picking up this book to read for the first time, never having heard of Pilsdon before; or reading this book again, having known Pilsdon for years, we hope that you find in it something both "refreshing" and "precious". Thousands of people owe more than can be said to people like yourself who have sustained us over the years by their interest and support.

## Acknowledgements

We are grateful for the kind permission of Anthony Russell (a member of the Community 1996-1997) for his drawing on page 141; to Paul Loebig for that on page 76; and to Valerie Baker for all other line drawings.

## PILSDON MORNING

'The first few years are the hardest' is a very true saying, and never more true than when setting up a modern community in a manor house in West Dorset.

Most, but by no means all, of the 'guests' were weighed down by an almost insupportable burden. Men and women, boys and girls, they came with problems of every kind – some labelled as psychotic and some tarred with the brush of social disgrace; some haunted by guilt, real or imaginary, and all of them unsure of themselves and their place in life.

Where else, and in what other circumstances, could men and women off the streets, from mental hospitals and prison cells, from schools and factories, universities and offices, teachers and tramps, bishops and knife-grinders, have all lived together?

For twenty years, the author Gaynor Smith with her husband Percy, built a community from nothing and gave home and comfort, work and a close-knit life to many hundreds of people. This, then, is the story of those first twenty years from 1958........

'..................And what you thought you came for
Is only a shell, a husk of meaning
From which the purpose breaks only when it is fulfilled
If at all.'
                              T.S. Eliot – *Little Gidding*

# PILSDON MORNING

Gaynor Smith

**PILSDON COMMUNITY**
**Bridport, Dorset**

*© Gaynor Smith, 1982*
*First published in Great Britain, 1982*
*Second Edition, 1999*

*For*
*RUTH*
*Who grew up with it*

*ISBN 0 9537199 0 1*
*Printed in England by Creeds the Printers, Bridport, Dorset*

# Contents

| | |
|---|---|
| Preface | 7 |
| Part One – The Place | 11 |
| Part Two – The People | 77 |
| Part Three – Big Box, Little Box | 129 |
| Epilogue | 138 |
| Postscript | 140 |

# Preface

I

"I won't! I won't! I won't!" she shouted as she stormed through the house banging each door behind her and finally collapsing in a heap on the sofa. On the train she had swallowed a whole bottleful of tablets and should have been dead but she had survived and arrived looking wraith-like, swaying on very high heels, painfully thin and almost transparent. She was hardly aware of what was going on around her. She drawled as she spoke and her eyes seemed out of focus. Drugs had taken a heavy toll.

He sat in a corner of the wide window seat trying to look as though he were invisible and shaking in every limb like a man in the grip of some terrible fever. His eyes were red-rimmed and watery and his skin blotchy and when he moved he seemed hardly able to drag himself across the room. Drink had robbed him of wife, children, home, profession, and seemed about to rob him of his life.

The man had arrived just before lunch. He had been let out of prison when the gates had opened at 7.30 that morning. His suit was dark and tidy but he had the grey look of a grey existence. He was nervy, unsure of himself, and unsure of his welcome, and still not quite adjusted to freedom. His eyes shifted uneasily. Before leaving he was given his railway ticket and came straight here. He had nowhere else to go.

Behind the trolley a young girl presided over the teapot. She was bright and friendly and exchanged a joke and a smile with most of the men and women who were collecting their cups of tea. Slim and attractive and dressed in the almost obligatory jeans and T-shirt she chatted cheerfully to her neighbour as she perched herself on the arm of the nearest chair. Who would have guessed she was the victim of a terrible agoraphobia that lay like a blight over her young life?

A middle-aged woman sat slumped in one of the armchairs by the fire, her face half hidden by greying hair falling across her forehead. Her handbag lay open at her feet. From time to time she picked it up and listlessly rummaged in its contents but there was nothing she wanted and presently it lay again discarded on the floor. Her skirt was long and brown and shapeless and there were two buttons missing from the top of her cardigan. She glanced furtively at her neighbours but refused to be drawn into any communication with them. Her life was a sea of unutterable loneliness and she was drowning in it.

The young man looked so ordinary. You would not have suspected him to be the victim of a terminal cancer that would soon ravage him. He was laughing and joking with a group of equally cheerful young people while another young man sat and strummed a guitar in the corner. Life was as normal for him as it was possible for it to be and the awareness of the cloud hanging over him was temporarily forgotten. The guitarist stopped playing and joined the group. So short a time ago he had been locked in his own angry rebellion and the despair of his parents and all who tried to help him, but now he was smiling as he approached the others. What were his own problems compared to the terrible isolating experiences of other men just as young as himself?

He looked big and strong but his speech was hesitant and slow and the slightly puzzled childlike look in his blue eyes hinted at a mind that was underdeveloped, and an inability to hold his own in a highly competitive and fast-moving world. He sat down and smiled at his neighbour but speech obviously did not come easily. He shifted his big frame in the chair, spread his hands out on his knees and stared at them. Once he looked up slightly sideways and again caught the eye of his neighbour and smiled rather sheepishly.

She was quite a young woman and a small boy stood beside her fingering the toggles on her duffle coat. The fourth finger of her left hand wore the plain gold band of marriage but the fingers of her right hand played with it and rubbed it up and down in an unconsciously symbolic gesture of uncertainty. Her face, although pretty, looked strained and she spoke impatiently to the child. How was she to know what to do, whether to try yet once more to patch up her difficult marriage or whether to break it once and for all? There would be time to think here but how was she to decide what to do? Out in the garden a mother and father and three children were all romping on the grass and their shouts of happy laughter brought a furrow between her eyes and tensed the muscles in her face. What help would she get here with her problem?

He had turned in out of the rain the previous night, a well-built man perhaps in his late thirties but with thinning hair and a noticeable absence of teeth. He was sitting with a group of rather older men and was chatting away to them. He seemed to know them well. His clothes were old and shabby, his shirt collar badly frayed, and the soles of his shoes had long since parted company with the uppers. But his eyes had twinkled last night as he ploughed his way through a mountain of bread and cheese and endless cups of strong tea. Would he stay long enough to remember what it was like to be a part of normal society or would his roving ways allow him only a brief acquaintance with the rituals of social living and the comforts of clean sheets and a hot bath?

All these, and hundreds more, were our friends at Pilsdon.

Few people know anything of community life: not much has been written about it and even less published, and the little that is known is mostly slanted, garbled, and lacking true authenticity, but there are probably over 500 communities in existence in this country alone and if we allow an average of 50 people in each that brings the total number of men, women, and children living in community up to 25,000 — as many people as there are living in a town about the size of Dover — and these people are not there because they have been forced into that kind of life but because they have voluntarily chosen it and because they like it and respond to its particular brand of culture.

Pilsdon was my home for twenty hears. It is a modern-style, mixed community of men, women, and children and in David Clark's authoritative book about communities called *Basic Communities* published by the S.P.C.K. it is classified as a 'caring' community, because not only does it offer a shared communal life but it also tries to help and rehabilitate people who are carrying an insupportable burden — drink, drugs, depression, a broken or breaking marriage, mental instability, inadequacy, loneliness, and total failure to conform to some pressurized pattern.

At first we were ill-equipped to deal with all the problems which came our way. Our doors were open day and night so that anyone who turned to us for help could find it, but sometimes the difficulties outweighed our capacity to handle them. It was not exactly a picnic hauling back into the house someone who had taken an overdose and crawled out into a muddy field to die, nor was it funny when a man who had taken it into his head to have a bike ride at 5.30 in the morning knocked up one of our neighbours, blood dripping from his knee to his ankle. And there was no relaxing when two men had quarrelled violently and were spoiling for a fight. Fortunately nobody murdered anybody and there were no fatal overdoses but it was sometimes a fairly near miss. Many of our neighbours looked askance at us; we were always the first port of call for the police investigating suspicious activities in the neighbourhood; our doctors tore their hair over us, and even the normally friendly ambulance men groaned a little as they came out to fetch yet another half-conscious body. Our resources were slim but we struggled on. Why? Because Pilsdon became a unique experience of friendship. Where else in the world could we have shared our lives with men and women from behind prison bars, from the locked wards of mental hospitals, from the streets and from doss houses, from every occupation — and unoccupation — and class and creed in society? Tinker, tailor, soldier, sailor, rich man, poor man, beggar man, thief — they were all at Pilsdon and they all contributed to this experience. It was something which grew up between us, gaining strength with the years and surviving all the stresses and strains imposed on it.

The story of Pilsdon then is the story of this unique friendship, it was this which was to become its heart and nerve centre and came to constitute its real ethos for all of us, and particularly perhaps for those men and women who had tasted all too little of it in their lives and some of whom were cynical about its very existence. For those who found in Jesus their inspiration this was an extension of that reality, but it was also something which could be shared by those who had no religious allegiance. We all came to know friendship not just as a spontaneous affinitive eruption between two people but as a way of life the basis of which was an unconditional acceptance. All of us, whether nominally Christian or not, were concerned with this ideal and with trying to break down, or through, the barriers so often created by wealth, status, education, culture, and even the barrier implicit in the word Christian.

If, like so many others, we were looking for some new direction in all the confusion of ideologies both inside and outside the Church, we were looking not so much for a new religious language or symbolism as for a new medium of communication, and we found this medium not in any belief in election or selection or any other form of privilege but in a shared experience of real or potential weakness and frailty. In spite of all our failures — and they were legion — written deeply into the heart of Pilsdon was the concept of the survival of the weakest — 'A bruised reed shall he not break, and the smoking flax shall he not quench'. We knew we were all in one way or another bruised reeds and it was in this knowledge of shared vulnerability that our friendships deepened and our humanity grew. Perhaps, too, it is a concept which the world is in fairly desperate need of today.

However, friendship is not all high heroics like the end of *A Tale of Two Cities* or Titus Oates walking out into the snow to die, nor does it always appear even to have much emotional content. It has a practical down-to-earth aspect and this is, in the main, a practical down-to-earth story. It deals with sickles and scythes, with pigs and cows, with pots and pans and bricks and mortar. If friendship was the wheel then these were the all-important spokes. And, because it is a very human story, it tells of the times when friendship flew out of the window and hostility and aggression flew in, with the times when friendship froze and the thread of acceptance wore treacherously thin.

The tale is not finished. Pilsdon is still a living venture. But I am writing about how it all started, first of all in our minds, and then how the dream took form and shape in an old house in West Dorset between the hills and the sea, how it grew, and changed a little in the growing, and what it came to mean to us all.

# Part One

## The Place

## II

Going, going, gone. The hammer fell with uncompromising finality and the house was ours, all twenty rooms of it together with a cottage and 9½ acres of land.

The large house went for a song. It seems unbelievable now that £5,000 paid for a manor house, enough land for a smallholding, and the two farm cottages used as one which was known as Bill's Cottage. Who the mythical Bill was we never discovered but he was probably one of the tenant farmers in the days when the whole estate comprised over 800 acres and was apportioned out among five farms.

We had gone to the auction with uncertain hopes, fearful that there might be someone as eager as us but much better equipped with funds bidding against us, fearful through ignorance of the actual nature and possibilities of an auction, and even fearful of success. It was a hazardous undertaking and how did we know that success at the sale itself might not spell disaster for us in the weeks and months to follow?

Three months before this fine October day a man called Mr Woods from New Zealand had made an offer for the entire estate. Our hopes had been shattered by a letter from the estate agents telling us of this. However a telephone call from the gentleman himself had dispelled the worst of our gloom. He informed us that his only interest was in the land and if we would care to rent the manor house he would be pleased to come to some amicable arrangement with us. Although this was not entirely satisfactory from our point of view as we wanted enough land to envisage the possibility of being self-supporting, the house seemed so right in every other way that we jumped even at this whittled-down chance of being its prospective inhabitants.

There began a seemingly endless and mystifying transaction between Mr Woods's solicitor and ours to reach an agreement as to the amount and clauses of the rent; all of which, to our great delight, proved abortive as Mr Woods later decided to lose interest in the whole business and we heard from the estate agents again that the estate was being divided up into lots which would be sold off by auction at the George Hotel, Axminster, on October 16th. The only other person whom we knew had been interested in the property was Sir Anthony Eden. He had apparently investigated the possibilities of a purchase but rumour had it that either his doctor or his bailiff had counselled him against it and we had no reason to suppose that he had any continuing interest in the place.

So here we were at the auction bidding for Lot 1 which comprised the seventeenth century manor house, an overgrown but potentially attractive walled garden, an orchard, a large grassy courtyard behind the house surrounded on the three remaining sides by stone outhouses, a medieval looking barn with slit windows and loose boxes backing onto a solid semicircular retaining wall. In addition to all this there was a sizeable field, and Bill's cottage separated from the field by a narrow country lane, and a stream the banks of which were soon, in spring, to be a mass of wild daffodils, little sisters of the larger golden-trumpeted garden variety.

We had first seen this feudal island in the late afternoon of a February day, tucked away in a corner of the little frequented and virtually unknown Marshwood Vale, a small area of West Dorset lying at the foot of Pilsdon Pen, its highest point, and far enough west to be almost on the borders of Devon. On the other side is the Wessex of Thomas Hardy, the landscape of 'Far from the madding crowd', the strange prehistoric forts and barrows of Eggardon and Maiden Castle, and in front is the sea with the small coastal towns of West Bay, Charmouth, and Lyme Regis which owes at least some of its fame to being the setting for both Jane Austen's *Persuasion* and more recently John Fowles's *The French Lieutenant's Woman.*

A little behind and to the east of Pilsdon lies Racedown House where Wordsworth once lived, and Blackdown, which looked to me when I first saw it a slightly dark and sinister spot. Beside the road was a small, burnt-out chapel and the area was heavily shrouded in trees. This is not surprising as there was once a forest here, Blackdown Forest, and it must then have been still more densely wooded. However, the little roadside chapel has now been rebuilt and its rather strange modern spire looks incongruous but neither grim nor foreboding.

To the south of Pilsdon Pen, and at its foot, the land drops into a hollow cup of copse and pasture land which is where the house is situated. And on the other side of this cup the land rises again gently to the great chalk cliffs which border the English Channel. The highest point of these cliffs, and it is the highest point on the whole south coast of England, is Golden Cap to the east of Charmouth, but the whole escarpment dropping to the sea along this coast is both dangerous and highly dramatic culminating as it does in the almost savage cliff scenery at Purbeck.

This then is the remote bit of West Dorset in which we found Pilsdon Manor. It must be one of the most rural areas in Britain, beautiful peaceful country unspoilt as yet by summer visitors or by commercialism of any kind. The kingfisher, shyest of birds, was still flitting up and down the stream when we first came to live there and many people have heard the nightingales singing in one of the copses near Whitchurch Canonicorum. The Vale boasts no factory or heavy industry of any kind, no railway, a bus only on Wednesdays and Saturdays, no ribbon development, no high-rise buildings, no motorway, and perhaps most important of all, no National Trust land heavily labelled 'Beauty Spot'. This does not mean that it is not beautiful but its beauty is of the quiet unassuming kind which hits no high sensual heights but lays a gentle finger on the heart and mind and gradually wins converts even amongst those who think they prefer the wild or the rugged or lush.

Pilsdon Pen, its highest point, stretches out its arms towards the tree-crowned hill of Lewesdon on one side and the more open slopes of Lambert's Castle on the other. They shelter the valley from the north although the winds sometimes seem to get trapped inside the basin so that their force is accentuated. The Pen itself is hardly even a mountain being only just over 900 feet high but when you climb up from its south side on a windy day and stand on the top bracing yourself against a strong gale you could well be 2,000 feet up because of its exposed position and the wide views of the surrounding countryside.

At the foot of the Pen, lying in the bottom of the cup before the land rises again towards the coast, is the manor house itself. You come steeply down from a road which skirts the forehead of the hill. There is now a car park at the top and a sign which says Pilsdon but the road down is still very narrow and, in winter, snow and ice often make it unnavigable, while in summer, the burgeoning hedges seem to clasp hands to prevent easy descent. About half-way down, the hill becomes less steep and there is a sharp turning to the right. Here too there is a signpost but if it is dark or you are too occupied with the view and miss this bend it may take you as much as another hour to find your way back to the house. But if you have been lucky or observant enough to follow the guiding arm, a tiny stream bordering the road will soon bring you right to the house itself.

It is not perhaps one of the most beautiful of the Dorset manor houses. It stands tall and rather severe, its three storeys, on the front, unbroken by any projecting ledges or buttresses. At the back the roof slides down further and a few dormer windows peep from its slopes, but the whole is too stiff and uncompromising for real beauty. It has no imposing entrance: the front and back doors are indistinguishable. It is built of ham stone and flint and the slates, substituted on the roof for stone tiles, have done nothing to improve its appearance. But the front windows are large and look out onto a walled garden and, particularly on a fine sunny day, the house looks pleasant in a slightly austere way.

Behind the house are all the ramifications of a large farm and country house — stables, loose boxes, solid stone sheds, a large grassy quadrangle and, almost most beautiful of all, an old tithe barn with the traditional slit windows. And in front of the house, if you step through an archway in the garden wall, is a small chapel the history of which nobody any longer seems to know. Whether it was originally attached to the manor house itself or to an older manor which may have stood on the same site, or whether it was a chapel of ease in the great see of Sherborne, is a matter of conjecture, but certainly it was there before the present house although its antiquity has been made less obvious by a fairly drastic renovation carried out in the latter part of the Victorian era. Nevertheless, their solid attempts at reconstruction have not been able to disguise the fact that the original walls are crooked, in order as tradition has it, to hoodwink the devil and make it difficult for him to find the altar. There is now, at the back of the church, a beautifully printed scroll giving the names of the rectors of Pilsdon, the first being Nicholas de ? Somerton and the date being 1319, so that the church is possibly about three hundred years older than the house, the latter being listed as early Jacobean.

Like the church the house is almost anonymous. There seems to be a conspiracy of silence about it. All that is known is that it was originally the seat of the Hody and Wyndham families and there is a curious story that King Charles, while fleeing to the coast, was thought to be hiding in it. Here his enemies came looking for him and being unable to find him, thought he might be dressed up as one of the maidservants and so proceeded not only to ransack the house but also to examine the unfortunate girls. Here the story ends and there seem to be no more, not even a glimpse of floating white draperies or the sound of a clanking chain.

Around the house and its gardens and orchard are a few solitary farmhouses and that is all there is of Pilsdon now, no hamlet, no village shop, no post office, not even a pub. And this was the setting for the project we had in mind, something that had been lurking in the background of all our thinking for eight years, since the time we had visited England, on leave from Hong Kong, in 1950.

It was to this quiet valley that we came one afternoon in February 1958 after hearing that Pilsdon Manor was for sale. And it was here that we returned in October full of the pride and also the anxieties of ownership. There was so much to do. The house had been empty for over a year and when we first turned the water on at the mains jets squirted in all directions. Pipes had burst and the gutters and drains were full of debris. The large walled garden in front of the house was a hayfield, and the huge greenhouse reminded me of a dilapidated Crystal Palace. But we set to work with a will, first scything down the long grass and scrubbing the inside of the house from top to bottom and, when all the papers had been duly signed and our ownership ratified, we lit the Aga in the kitchen, imported a well-scrubbed plain deal table, almost our only piece of furniture, and sat down for our first meal together.

We were a strange little company. There was Percy, and Ruth our daughter, and myself, and Gillian who had left her comfortable home at Westhay in Hawkchurch to join in what was certainly at first a spartan community existence. Bill Burn had sold his cottage in Kent in the autumn of the previous year and had also come to live with us. He was a linguist and a historian as well as being a clever handyman who restructured part of the library ceiling. He was a bachelor of the Mr Chips kind with a very old Austin called Aggie and a small corgi called Tig. Aggie was a major hazard for the passenger. One day Bill and I went out delivering leaflets. I have forgotten what the leaflets were all about but I do remember that it was raining hard and water came spurting up at me from the floorboards and slid down my neck from the roof and squirted at my left arm from the window. Probably the same thing was happening to Bill but he seemed blissfully unaware of any discomfort.

Pippo was also with us. He was a young man from a small village somewhere in Italy who wanted to learn English but found the strange circumstances of our life quite beyond his comprehension and was not with us long. And Kenneth was starving himself to death through loneliness but was rescued by his doctor and sent to Pilsdon where we fed him at first exclusively on porridge and cold baked beans — the only two things he would eat. Later cold macaroni cheese was added to the diet.

That first meal together was jacket potatoes and baked beans. They tasted good. We were a community, albeit a tiny one, and our community life had begun. In the afternoon we lit a huge fire in what later became the dining-room and sat on the floor, we held our bread to the flames and had hot buttered toast washed down with great mugfuls of tea. There was no furniture then but the previous owners had left behind a large framed picture of a naked lady sitting on what looked like a marble bath. She was trying to keep herself warm with her long, rather faded, auburn hair but the attempt looked abortive and we later, with unconscious irony, consigned her to the incinerator.

We had only been living at Pilsdon for about a week when suddenly, out of the blue, appeared what seemed like dozens of reporters and photographers all wanting to know why we had bought the manor house and what we were going to do with it. Communities are not set up every day of the week and the interest was understandable, but it quickly escalated from purely local to national proportions and the crowning achievement was a full-scale account of all our doings which occupied the whole of the two centre pages of the *Daily Mirror*. It was accompanied by a picture of Percy and myself looking far from glamorous: Percy was in wellington boots and an old pullover and the caption read 'Parson in wellington boots' as though no parson had ever worn wellington boots before.

The write-up was not wholly a misinterpretation of our life but was sufficiently indeterminate for us to get letters subsequently asking us to do such varied things as bail men out of prison, arrange marriages for unlikely partners, and provide a holiday home for lonely people with their dogs, cats, and canaries. Perhaps it was our own fault. What we were doing had no very clear-cut boundaries or definitions: at the beginning Pilsdon was feeling its way into its own pattern and purpose.

Undoubtedly Percy originally saw Pilsdon very much in terms of Little Gidding and the ordered liturgy of the Church. But this aspect of the community, although deeply precious to some, was not shared by all so that what did become perhaps the major, and certainly both the most obvious and for many of us the most fulfilling, side of Pilsdon life was its concern with the welfare of its 'guests', most of whom were men and women with a problem of one kind or another, who were battling to try and find a way out of their own particular mental and emotional jungles; people who had ground to a halt and needed a shortish or longish respite from the pressures of their daily lives.

Pilsdon is very much off the beaten track but immediately they started coming. This is the year of the disabled but the disabled in our society are not only the physically handicapped or the mentally retarded or maladjusted but also those whose minds and nerves and bodies are breaking under the strain of inner and outer tension, who are engaged in a fruitless and frustrating search for meaning in the maze of modern life. 'Everyone has a threshold of endurance beyond which he cannot go without breaking.' Percy wrote that in his Christmas letter to the community and all its friends in 1962, and those who are forced beyond their own theshold are disabled. There were, and are, many people at Pilsdon like that. They found their way, slowly at first, but in ever increasing numbers. We were astonished by the demand and gradually had to adjust ourselves to coping with it.

There are people who feel that conditions in our world are so bad now that to try and ameliorate them a little by welfare work may cloak the real problem and possibly even hinder effective large-scale action. But if you see a man lying in the road after a car accident you do not leave him lying there and say 'We must pass a Traffic Act'. You do something about him. You may still try to get a traffic act passed but you have also done something about an injured man. Hospitals have a Casualty Department as well as research laboratories where the deeper and wider issues of medicine are studied, and solutions to some of its problems both found and then practised. Both are necessary and if, for some of the people who came to us, we were only a 'casualty department' we were like people on the street witnessing an accident, and you do not pass by on the other side. The trouble comes when you start thinking the casualty department, because it is so immediate, is the most important part of the hospital. And of course it is not. But first aid is still necessary, and invaluable as far as it goes.

But, more important than the welfare work we were doing, was what grew between us. It was the humanity, wide in its scope and fascinating in its diversity, that brought people to Pilsdon who would normally never have darkened the doors of a 'religious' community, and brought them back time and time again to share our life and experiences.

And the sharing was real. The friendships that grew were not based on patronage but on involvement. Whatever had brought us all to Pilsdon, we identified with one another each of us knowing in our heart of hearts that 'there, but for the grace of God, go I'.

And we all learnt from one another. The detachment that is often, at least officially, expected of the welfare worker was not ours. We were involved in each other's lives. We were not dispensing charity but the blood and sweat of our hearts and bodies. We gave and received in equal measure and it was this experience of equality, of sharing, of baptism into the lives of others which was essentially 'the Pilsdon experience'.

## III

We have often been asked why we founded Pilsdon, what drove us to step aside from the more familiar and conventional paths of work and family life and out on to uncharted seas towards an unknown destination.

I do not know when Pilsdon really began. It depends so much on whether you believe in what is called determinism or whether you think each moment is an independent self-governing body or whether you manage to thread your way through a rather elusive mixture of both. But certainly nothing starts where it seems to start: the water does not suddenly begin where the stream appears above ground.

It is not unusual for men and women who are religious in adolescence to be attracted by the ideal of the older-style religious communities. The Church has, over the centuries, cultivated the belief that monks and nuns are somehow a race apart, and a little above, the rest of us. If you are going to strive for holiness or want to live your religion every day of the week as well as Sunday, this is probably the best path. It will have its dangers and difficulties but the route is mapped out and the signposts are clear.

Both Percy and I were religious teenagers. He was not brought up in a church-going family but was converted to Christianity by his science master who held Bible study groups in his home in the evenings and combined it with the attractions of table tennis and snooker. He then started attending the services of an Anglo-Catholic church at Leigh-on-Sea where he lived and was further influenced deeply and permanently by the vicar of the parish. It is not altogether surprising that, in spite of a very ordinary and human interest in girls, the idea and ideals of monasticism should have taken root in Percy's mind and that it should have appeared to be the highest Christian aspiration even if apparently intended only for the few. It is also not surprising that, after leaving school and going to work as a clerk in the Bank of England, he should one day have felt called to become a priest, that he left the Bank and became an undergraduate at St Edmund Hall, Oxford. It was there, in the spring of 1941, that we met.

I too was then religiously inclined. I had been nurtured in it from my earliest years. My father was a Welsh Presbyterian minister and had the care of a chapel in Rhyl on the North Wales coast for the last thirty years of his life. He was a beloved pastor, a sincere and ardent preacher, a widely-read and liberal theologian, a man with a simple faith but a broad intelligence — a good man.

My mother found faith more difficult but she never deviated from the outward forms and my sister and I were brought up to attend services three times on Sunday — my chief delight when I was small being a vast and beautiful chandelier which hung from the ceiling in the centre of the chapel and lighted the whole building — and the Band of Hope on Friday evenings. At the Band of Hope we were exhorted to remember the deadly perils of alcohol and to renounce it for ever, and our imaginations were further assisted by lurid tales of forsaken children waiting sadly for their parents outside public houses, and poverty-stricken homes. Little did I dream at the time that I should one day see a great deal more of the effects of this 'peril'.

For some reason, and I do not blame my parents, I was an insecure child and a still more insecure adolescent, and I turned more and more to the strength and comfort offered by this tradition in which I had been brought up. So it was that, by the time Percy and I met in 1941, we were both what most people would describe as very religious, although we preferred the term spiritual, meaning I think by this distinction that we were interested not so much in morals, nor in the dogmas and doctrines of the church, nor in evangelism, nor in any legalism about church attendance, but in the search for a direct, unmediated experience of God and of his controlling power in our lives. We both dreamed of religious communities, read the lives of those who had lived in them, and dedicated ourselves to the spiritual life. No knights of the Grail could have been more earnest in their quest. The founding of Pilsdon was still nearly twenty years away but the journey which led us there had begun.

1950 was the year that finally saw our lives turn dramatically from conventional paths to the very unconventional one of founding a modern, mixed, religious community.

We had been living in Hong Kong for four years. Percy was ordained deacon in the Church of England in the summer of 1946 and almost immediately afterwards we set sail for the Far East where, for one year, we both taught in St Paul's School, a large co-educational school for Chinese children. Percy was also chaplain to the Cathedral and was helping to reorganize the work of the boys' and girls' clubs in the poorer areas of the city. For this he was well qualified. He was a pacifist and his war work had consisted first of driving an ambulance in London and then of running a Youth Club in Somers Town before going up to Westcott House in Cambridge to study theology in 1944.

Percy had always wanted to go to China and he revelled in the new sights and sounds and friendships. But I sat, when I could, at the big window of our sitting-room, half-way up the Victoria Peak, and gazed with home-sick eyes at the ships coming and going in the beautiful harbour below. I was afraid of the unknown strangeness and although we lived in Hong Kong for seven years I was never to overcome this fear and sense of alienation.

However there was work to do. The war had recently ended and the colony was free again but during the Japanese occupation little had gone on in the way of education and the children we taught were eager to learn and to make up for lost time. Teaching them was easy and rewarding and, if there was a certain challenge missing, it was compensated for by the difficulties of understanding and being understood. As I was a trained English teacher I had the two top classes and one of the set books they were studying was the last chapter of *Tom Brown's Schooldays*. This is a detailed and long-winded account of a cricket match and as none of them had ever seen the game played — some of them had never even heard of it — my near-desperate attempts to explain to them the meanings of such terms as lob, and yorker, and silly mid-off and square leg, met with uncomprehending astonishment.

After a year we moved across to the mainland of Kowloon and Percy was given charge of one of the English-speaking churches, Christ Church in Kowloon Tong. Here there was even more work for him. The church had been used as stables by the Japanese during the war and was stripped bare: only the roof and walls remained. So, on half a salary, Percy set about reassembling a congregation and refurnishing the church. This pioneering work has always been Percy's forte: consolidation may bore him but the spade work excites and stimulates. This trait in his character and this experience in Kowloon were to serve him in good stead when, ten years later, he brought into being the community now known as Pilsdon.

It was not long before the church was again a flourishing centre and was supported by a loyal and generous congregation of English-speaking Chinese, Eurasians, Americans, and Europeans. But in 1950, for six months, work was set aside and we sailed for England with our two-year-old daughter, Ruth, landing there on a bitingly cold snowy morning in March.

To me, in retrospect, this holiday has been blurred by sadness. My father had died while we were in Hong Kong and this was to be the last time I was to see my mother: she died soon after our return to Kowloon. But the often denigrated English climate was wonderful after the stifling humidity of Hong Kong and, after two bouts of malaria, I was badly in need of this refreshment. Ruth however was unsettled by the change of environment and cried bitterly for her home and Percy gradually grew restless and was anxious to be back at work.

We returned to Kowloon in October and we took with us as reading material for the journey a book I had found in Mowbray's bookshop in London. It was called *Nicholas Ferrar of Little Gidding*. A casual glance inside told me it was a book about a community founded in the seventeenth century by a man called Nicholas Ferrar and Pilsdon took its first conscious breath with the finding of this book. It is often such apparently trivial things — the opening of a door, the flicking over of the pages of a book — that have momentous consequences for us. Without knowing it we were nearing the big turning point of our lives.

Little Gidding is the name of a small hamlet in Huntingdonshire which is now just off the A1. It was there in 1625 that a young man called Nicholas Ferrar went, with his mother and a sister and brother both of whom were married and had children. Nicholas was then thirty-three, a Member of Parliament and Deputy Treasurer of the Virginia Company. Very few of his friends could understand why he wanted to renounce all this in favour of burying himself in a remote and isolated manor house in the heart of the country. Here you may begin to detect a slight parallel and it is an interesting aside that Mrs Ferrar bought the very dilapidated manor house at Little Gidding for £6,000 whereas we, more than 300 years later, only paid £5,000 for a manor house in good repair. But Nicholas's mind was made up. He wanted to live and work and worship in a small community and serve all who came to it. Here the parallel becomes still clearer. The household soon numbered thirty people, men, women, and children. Isaac Walton of angling fame called it a 'little college' and George Herbert, the poet, loved its quiet peacefulness. For twelve years Nicholas led and inspired this community and it continued for another twenty years after his death and during all that time a constant stream of guests came to Little Gidding for refreshment of body, mind, and spirit.

This is the story that inspired T. S. Eliot's poem 'Little Gidding' and it was this story that set our feet on the trail that led to Pilsdon. We felt we wanted to take up the thread that was forcibly dropped in 1657 and reanimate an ideal which had been given life for only thirty-two years just three hundred years before we read of it. Percy's whole being assented to the way of life that had existed at Little Gidding and his mind and heart were fired by the personality of Nicholas Ferrar himself. Here was a possible ideal, a life that was almost monastic but surrounded by the family and offering help to all who needed it. This was monasticism with a difference, a difference which made it a viable way of life for a married man in the twentieth century. Would it be possible to start again where this community had left off? Could we give up all the conventional ideas about family life and start out on an unknown road towards an unknown future?

Three things helped to point us towards our decision.

In 1951, soon after our return to Hong Kong, my mother died and I suffered so severely from the shock of this that, but for Percy's unceasing and wholly dedicated care and attention, I might well have found myself in the hands of a psychiatrist. Hong Kong had never been home to me and now I felt more alienated from it than ever, cut off in a land of strangers from my roots, from my securities, and from my permanent realities. It was obvious that I was fairly desperately in need of a return to a way of life that was familiar and homely and beloved.

Percy on the other hand was in love with all things Chinese but perhaps some change was indicated for him too. The first pioneering work at Christ Church was over: the church was flourishing, with a strong settled congregation and financial stability. But the parishioners numbered twenty-five thousand and Percy was finding the routine visits of an ordinary parish priest quite inadequate to deal with the troubles and problems that beset such a vast number of people. The Anglican parish system seemed ludicrously inept. He felt he wanted to give more time and energy to a few of the problems instead of dissipating his time and energies over so many. Also he yearned for companionship in the daily performing of the services of the church, Holy Communion, Matins, Evensong, and Compline.

And the last determining factor was the words of a friend, Erik Kvan, a Danish priest living in Hong Kong. He was sitting in our garden with Percy and the conversation had come round to the book which had made such a deep impression on us — the story of Little Gidding. Erik knew the story and was in sympathy with the idea of community living — he lived in one himself for some years out in the New Territories — and perhaps some intuition in him voiced Percy's thoughts as he turned to him and said:

"Why don't you start a community on the same lines?"

I do not remember discussing the matter very much: I think Percy's decision had been made after reading of the Little Gidding community. It nearly broke his heart to think of leaving Hong Kong but the pointer was set and his mind was made up, so in 1953 we left China and set sail for England there to found a community on the lines of Little Gidding but with the changes and adjustments that would be necessary from attempting to do the same kind of thing in the twentieth century. I do not think Percy at that time realized how very great that change would have to be and how different from Little Gidding Pilsdon would eventually become. We no longer live in an age of faith or of universally accepted traditions and social patterns: everything is in flux and there is no knowing what life will be like when and if the turbulence eventually settles. But this is how things were for us at the beginning: what they became is the rest of the story.

We landed on English soil again in 1954 and immediately made a personal pilgrimage to Huntingdonshire to see the church at Little Gidding and the graves of Nicholas and John Ferrar. By now there is again a community at Little Gidding — it is an age of communities — but then there was nothing but the deserted chapel and the solitary gravestones. It was eerily silent.

For eight months after this we enjoyed an extended holiday keeping a weather eye open for any traces of a large house and chapel which might be empty and awaiting our occupation. We rented two cottages, one in Cornwall and one in Oxfordshire, and travelled the length and breadth of the country in our search, but every large house was either occupied or wholly ruined or too urban for our liking. We had already decided that our experiment must have a rural setting: we had lived in a very large town for nearly eight years and we both felt that our community must be nearer the soil and well away from the sophistications of urban life. However, after six months, having found nothing that seemed to answer our need, we decided we had better settle for parish work again: funds were running short and perhaps our enthusiasm for our venture was also at a low ebb. So, after a two months' search, Percy accepted the living of Hawkchurch in Devon, little suspecting that the perfect house for our community was lying almost at our feet, six miles away in the Marshwood Vale.

It was to be another three and a half years before we heard of Pilsdon and then in strange circumstances. Percy was attending a meeting of the clergy of the area when he heard that Pilsdon church would have to be closed because of lack of support both personal and financial. This news however made little impression on him until he was returning home and visited an elderly friend. She knew of Percy's interest in Little Gidding and also had the story of it on her shelves. Was it accidental or by design that she then told him that Pilsdon Manor was for sale? We shall never know as she has been dead for many years and we never thought of asking her. But it was a match to the tinder: Pilsdon Manor for sale — Pilsdon church about to be shut. And as we drove steeply down the Pen road the evening of that same day I think we knew before arriving that this was going to be journey's end — journey's end and a journey's beginning. And when we rounded the bend and saw the little church with a steeple so incredibly like the one at Little Gidding there could be no doubt in our minds that this was to be the scene for the re-enacting of a long forgotten vision.

But the long wait was not yet over. We had seen the right house and it was for sale but how many other people thought it was also the right house for them? What we thought we wanted and what we were going to be allowed to have were not necessarily the same thing. Funds were running low: the death of both my parents had left us with a small amount of capital but it was not enough to buy a house, let alone a large manor house set in 9½ acres of land.

So Percy drafted a letter about what we were hoping to do, mentioning Little Gidding and our plans to set up a community on something the same lines: a group of men and women living and working together and offering help and hospitality to all those, burdened and unburdened, who might care to share this life with us. This letter was then sent round to all our friends and relatives asking for whatever financial help they felt they could give, either as a loan or as an outright gift. This was the only time in all the years we were at Pilsdon that we ever asked for money. We never again had to beg for financial support. But the generosity that was to follow was already on its way and gradually our dwindling capital was inflated and we began to feel that we might be able to make some kind of reasonable offer for the house.

Two days after that memorable evening when we first saw Pilsdon Manor we had gone to Sherborne to see the estate agents, Rawlence and Squarey. We met Mr Rawlence himself and explained to him why we wanted to acquire the manor house and what we were hoping to do there. He was sympathetic and listend to our story patiently but I wondered what private opinion he was forming of two people who must have sounded like harmless lunatics harbouring illusions of grandeur.

Then came the long months of waiting, with money dribbling in and our vision gradually being shared with other people. Michael and Betty Pinney who live in the neighbouring manor house at Bettiscombe were full of enthusiasm for the project and gave us unqualified support both then and later when the dream was becoming a reality. And Gillian, who was to be the first permanent community member, had already committed herself to the venture.

Percy was still at this time the vicar of Hawkchurch and was to remain so until the end of January 1959 although we had started living at Pilsdon on the first day of the new year. When Percy told Bishop Anderson, the then bishop of Salisbury, what we were planning to do, he was cautious, outlined many potential snags and objections, and would only consent to the venture if Percy gave up entirely being vicar of Hawkchurch and devoted his whole time and energies to Pilsdon. The bishop was a Scot and his caution may have been temperamental but, for us, this meant the cutting of our last link with any kind of salary or financial security. We were about to plunge into deep water and there were to be no lifebelts.

Many people prophesied disaster — not even our closest friends gave it more than a few years, or even months. We were proposing to live without any regular source of income and very little opportunity for future employment if things went wrong. But October 16th found Percy and Gillian and myself in one of the rooms of the George Hotel, Axminster. The great day of the auction had come.

## IV

"We're thinking of starting a community something on the lines of Pilsdon. Could you tell us what snags to look out for and how to cope with them?"

The couple raised quizzical eyebrows in my direction and waited for some penetrating and useful advice.

"If you think about the snags before you start you'll never get going at all. Just plunge in and take what comes."

Well, we had plunged, and life at Pilsdon was fast gathering momentum. More and more people were coming, some to give help, some to receive it, and some just out of curiosity. Furniture too big for the average modern house or flat came trundling up the drive — huge wardrobes, a massive sideboard, tables, chairs, cutlery, crockery, and a meat dish that looked large enough for a royal banquet. Generosity knew no bounds and it was not long before the house was fully furnished and our first cow, Susannah, was standing in the cow shed meekly demanding attention.

Pilsdon in those days was tough and spartan. There was no central heating and no mains electricity. The rooms were cold and draughty in winter and the corridors even worse. The windows did not fit properly and the floorboards gaped. We had no amenities, no washing machine, no electric fires, no electric mixer, not even an electric kettle. Percy and Ruth and I shared one very large room in an outside shed which later became the pottery, and the other community members only had a very small room to themselves. But we had plenty of good food, plenty of blankets and hot-water bottles, a beautifully warm Aga in the kitchen and, in winter, a roaring log fire in the sitting-room, a library of books, community cars to ride in and, in summer, wide lawns to sit on and a flower garden to enjoy. We worked hard but life was stimulating and exciting.

We aimed to become self-supporting. Susannah, our first cow, was the forerunner of a small herd of eight or ten. Most of these were Ayrshires or had some Ayrshire in them but we once had a lovely Jersey called Beauty and she was appropriately named. The only other cow whose name suited her was Passion. I privately thought she was a hermaphrodite: she had the thick heavy shoulders of a bull and a temper to match. Nobody could do anything with her and after she had brought two men to the ground we decided it was time for her to go. Many of the other cows had much more outlandish names. There were Bigger and Better, Straight and Narrow who were Jersey twins, and Marijuana, Belladonna, Hashish, Valium, and Cannabis. As we never kept a bull we had regular visits from the A.I. man and I do not know what he thought of such appellations — they must have told him more about the human population of Pilsdon than about the cows. Most of the time we sold our milk keeping back only enough for our own use, but at one time we kept it all and made butter with the cream and Blue Vinney cheese with the skimmed remainder. However we found this less profitable than the sale of milk.

The breeding of pigs was also a part of our economy but we could never quite bring ourselves to kill them so we fattened them for sale to Walls — which was only passing the buck. There was always someone detailed for pig duty and it never ceased to amaze me that the people who looked after the pigs grew so fond of them. Patrick could hardly be dragged away from them even at meal times. He would sit in the piggery, the potent smell of ammonia notwithstanding, and watch them and stroke their necks. They love this — pigs must be sensuous creatures. It sends them into a kind of trance: their eyes glaze, their knees buckle and they swoon against the nearest wall. We also had poultry in deep litter and sent hundreds of eggs away every week to the egg packing station at Crewkerne.

So, cows had to be milked and the cowstalls washed and scrubbed down twice a day; the dairy buckets and pans, skimmers and ladles had to be thoroughly cleaned and scoured after every milking; the pigsties had to be kept clean, the gilts weighed for sale, the litters provided with warm shelter, and an eye kept on the mother pig in case she fell ill or collapsed on too many of her offspring. The hens had to be fed, the eggs collected and washed and crated, and fresh straw put down on the floor of the henhouses. Electric fences had to be put up in the fields and kept in repair, bales of straw had to be humped about and large quantities of food lugged from grain store to pigsty, chicken house or milking parlour. And all around the house and farm hedges had to be cut, ditches cleared out and, in summer, the hay collected and stored. All this farming meant a considerable amount of work for everybody and most people thoroughly enjoyed it. Everyone loved watching the cows being milked by hand and the milk frothing into the big pails. And we all enjoyed the birth of the calves and sometimes being allowed to feed them. Townspeople sometimes shuddered initially at the thought of being licked by their furry tongues but they came to love it and we were all sad when the beautiful doe-eyed creatures had to go to market.

**Animals have a healing power.**

We had a dog, a border collie called Smog, who became a Pilsdon institution. His master had died and, being untrained in the proper arts of a sheep-dog, he was not wanted by any other farmer so he was brought to our door in the hope that we might befriend him. He had a loving nature but probably not a very high I.Q. and he quickly became too fat on biscuits and sandwiches surreptitiously stowed away at elevenses and tea-time and later stuffed into his ever-willing mouth. It was not a kindness and everyone was constantly reminded of this but there is something about an animal, even in zoos with explicit warning notices, which invites feeding — people perhaps feel this is their only point of contact with them — and Smog was no exception. But, as much of this book is about friendship, it would hardly be complete without the tale of Smog and Sandy. Sandy lived next door. He was an old English sheep-dog who was well trained and useful with his master's cows but all his spare time was spent with Smog. Smog never went to Sandy's house — he never left Pilsdon except to follow at the heels of Ruth's pony when she went out for a ride — but every day Sandy would come over to see Smog and together they would romp and roll on our grass. Later, when Smog had to be put down, Sandy came to Pilsdon once or twice and wandered dejectedly round the courtyard, then he never visited us again.

It was the winter of 1963 and bitterly cold when Mumpus strayed in. She was a beautiful long-haired tabby who stayed with us for about ten years. Although petted by many and affectionate with human beings — as much as a cat ever can be — she never became a lap cat but retained her slim figure and her killer instinct until her death. Also she had no time for strange dogs who came visiting with their masters. One day she found one imprudently invading her territory and flew at him so fast and so unexpectedly that she bowled him right over on the floor, after which he beat a hasty retreat with Mumpus spitting after him like a tigress. She killed countless rats and mice and reared countless families, hence her name Mum-puss, and always she retained her proud independence which might have been the envy of many a lesser cat.

We also had bees which were given to us and I once had the doubtful privilege of looking after them. If you like bees and know how to handle them I daresay the whole process may be quite enjoyable — it is certainly interesting as their life is a model of a well-organized community — but as I knew less than nothing about them I had regular visitations of panic right through the summer and got badly stung even when dressed up in my bee veil because the wind kept blowing both it and the clustered bees against my face and neck. Many a night I lay awake for hours thinking up ways of outwitting and outmanoeuvring their stinging propensities and, to my great relief, after I had battled with them for four years one of Pilsdon's most loyal friends, Stan Ewins, asked if I would like him to take care of our bees as well as his own and thankfully I folded up my veil.

But of such stuff is community living made.

Sentimentality about animals, certainly, was never encouraged at

Pilsdon — we were too serious a farming community for that — but animals and birds do have a way of stealing into people's hearts and making themselves remembered. Evelyn once rescued the runt of one of the litters and brought her up almost as a pet. Pigoletta came to meals with us one summer on the lawn and trotted round after her rescuer like a tiny dog. She was playful and endearing but I doubt whether she would have been the one, or Evelyn would have wanted her to be the other, when she weighed a solid three hundred pounds. We also had a pet hen called Harriet and there was a very tame but sad-looking blackbird who must have lived near. He had no feathers on his head or neck and we christened him Hiroshima. Our birds were all fairly tame though the wagtails who strutted about on the front lawn kept their distance, and a beautiful pair of goldfinches who nested every year in the garden were only a streak of gold in the sun. One of the loveliest sights I ever saw at Pilsdon was a great green woodpecker against a tree in the snow. I was almost near enough to touch him when I suddenly turned and there he was with his brilliant green feathers and red-capped head. I suppose the snow had muffled my footsteps and he seemed unaware of my presence as I enjoyed a long look at his emerald back. And we had beautiful white pigeons who nested in one of our old barns, but my love for them was not shared by the gardeners. Many attempts were made to exterminate them but to my joy and relief these attempts were never wholly successful and we always seemed to have a fresh crop of pigeons to replace the ones who, on one occasion, nearly became pigeon pie.

In addition to all our livestock we had a large vegetable garden which supplied us over the years with nearly all the vegetables we could eat, and a huge greenhouse in which the seedlings were sown and pricked out and where we grew tomatoes, cucumbers, peppers, and occasionally melons. There was plenty of space in the garden too for soft fruit, strawberries, raspberries, gooseberries, red currants and black currants, and an orchard with apple trees. And in front of the house was the beautiful walled garden with large lawns, wide herbaceous borders and beds of roses. It was no wonder that people soon started coming from miles around to visit us in the spring and summer and to walk round the house and grounds.

All this again meant much hard work, digging trenches, planting, weeding, hoeing, picking fruit and vegetables and preparing them for bottle, table, and saucepan and, much later, three deep freezers. Paths had to be weeded as well as flower beds and vegetable plots, the lawns kept neat and trim, and the edges clipped.

The house, too, was a sizeable manor house so this also had its own quota of work attached. Every morning everyone did some house work before going out to garden, barn, or field. There was cooking and washing, and always some extra jobs such as mending and sorting out the linen, and plastering, painting and plumbing. And outside the house was a vast collection of stone sheds, wooden loose boxes and barns and these needed conversion, retiling, and reridging.

Extra to all this run-of-the-mill daily work we always had some special project on hand. One of these was, in the early years, the conversion of some of the loose boxes into bedrooms and in this we were greatly helped initially by Rotarians from Lyme Regis who laid the floors. We then had more adequate accommodation for our growing number of guests. The rooms in the house, although very large, could not be sub-divided so they offered only dormitory sleeping space whereas the loose boxes held only one, or at most two people.

But one of the biggest jobs we tackled in those first years was the restoration of the church. In this we were following in the steps of Little Gidding and an age-old tradition of religious communities. Before we had come to Pilsdon this small but attractive old building had been virtually condemned so we set about strengthening and also beautifying it. The vestry and the south and east outside walls had to be completely repointed and a new floor laid on the south side of the aisle because the existing joists had almost rotted away. Much of the inside had to be replastered and in preparing the walls for this we discovered two small holy water stoups, presumably a relic of pre-Reformation days. The inside of the church was gloomy with pitch-pine pews painted and varnished a hideous dark brown, so with bits of broken glass and sandpaper we set about renovating it and restoring the wood to its natural colour. It was a mammoth task and took many months to complete and several tins of elastoplast. After the scraping was over we used our own beeswax to add a final polish and the result was quite unexpectedly beautiful.

All this work in the church we did ourselves with the help of the guests who were staying with us. But there was one job we could not tackle. The lead of all the windows had perished and much of the glass was cracked or broken so that we had to replace the windows, with the exception of the stained glass above the altar, and this was done by Wippells of Exeter in pure white English antique glass. But this employment of an outside firm was very much the exception at Pilsdon rather than the rule. Our aim to be self-supporting extended to maintenance and extension as well as produce and we usually managed to do everything ourselves, including the turning of loose boxes into bedrooms, a barn into a pottery and craft room, and two sheds into a large hall with a stage at one end and a minstrel's gallery at the back.

Work was very important to us. It was a vital and significant part of our life together. Most of us were young and energetic and needed it, and so did our guests. Also, Percy felt strongly that it gave a vigorous and healthy basis to our communal existence and gained us a respect which would not have been accorded to us had we been lazy or slovenly. So work was found for everyone and nobody stayed long at Pilsdon unless they were both able and willing to take their part in the many jobs that clamoured for attention. We all did everything there was to do, sharing in the work without distinction of rank or status. Percy himself milked the cows, dug the vegetable garden and cleaned out the drains, and doctors, writers, wayfarers, parsons, and businessmen all scrubbed down the pigsties and the milking sheds, cleared out ditches and learnt how to plant a straight line of cabbages. And, perhaps most significantly of all, nobody was paid a cent for their labour. We worked because there was no other way for the community to exist and we wanted it to exist so our work was our contribution to it. But this freeing of work from its usual associations with a pay packet, or the pay packet of other people, from its linkage with ambition and the drive for power, together with its obvious and immediate usefulness to the community, gave it a whole new dimension of meaning for many people and our life at Pilsdon a freedom and equality of relationships which might have been harder to achieve in any other way.

By this time many wayfarers had begun to find their way to Pilsdon and the work of repointing the church was done almost single-handed by Joe. He was an Irish wayfarer with a flair for the romantic. When he talked about 'the call of the wild' you felt your feet tingling and the rush of wind across your face, though his stories of poaching hardly equalled those of Bill who arrived at Pilsdon a few years later. However Joe was very much the star of our first television appearance. It was in May 1959 that the BBC decided to make a short documentary film of the community. Revd Austen Williams, Vicar of St Martin-in-the-fields, kindly consented to do the interviewing but Joe was the star turn. He talked easily and eloquently about life on the roads, about the lure of its freedom and its vagabond excitements. He was a distinguished-looking man with grey hair, a ruddy complexion, the almost startlingly blue eyes of the Irish, and a charm of manner that must have melted the defences of many a housewife when called upon for a loaf of bread and something hot for the 'wee drum'.

Like so many other men Joe came and went at Pilsdon for some years staying for about three or four months, suddenly disappearing one bright sunny morning and reappearing six or seven months later when a coating of frost at night might be beginning to make the hedge a less acceptable bed. Then there was a last stay and we never saw Joe again. It was rumoured that he had been seen in a pub in Torquay handing out £5 notes to all-comers so perhaps a win on the pools had changed his fortunes but it would have had to be a very big win indeed to have lasted long.

Several short films were made of Pilsdon in the first five or six years but the longest was made for Meeting Point in 1965. For this the film and camera crew were with us for four days and however careful and considerate a film-making team may be it is impossible to make a feature film of any length without considerable disruption to the life and activities of those concerned. One lunch-time took two hours to film and the soup had to be reheated several times in the process. We filed again and again into the dining-room and once when it had seemed as near perfect as it was ever going to be the whole scene was shattered by one man irreverently muttering "rhubarb, rhubarb, rhubarb" loudly under his breath, and we had to start all over again.

The film when it was made was the best and most comprehensive that was ever made of Pilsdon and yet to us who lived there it was strangely unsatisfying. I used to think that, had we had the technical know-how, we could have made a better one ourselves, perhaps a comedy series something on the lines of 'All creatures great and small'. It might have given a better picture of what our life was often like. Laughter never featured in any of the films they made about us and yet there was much fun at Pilsdon even in the midst of tension and strain.

One of the early Pilsdon projects was the market. The cultivation of the large vegetable garden had been a priority right from the beginning and by 1962 we had enough extra produce to make it a viable proposition to sell some of it at a market stall in Axminster. So every Thursday two people set off after breakfast for the market laden not only with vegetables and soft fruit but also with gingerbread and flapjacks which were the kitchen's contribution to the sale.

Hours of hard labour were needed to make this possible. The vegetables had to be not only grown, and grown well, but they had to be lifted from the ground, or picked, and trimmed and washed thoroughly before they were fit for their public appearance on the stall. We usually did the selling in twos changing over at lunch-time, the second pair then holding the fort either until the market closed at about 4.30 p.m. or until everything was sold out if that happened sooner. And this sale of our goods went on right through the summer and autumn of 1962, but when winter came we closed down the stall and after the Great Snow of 1963 nobody had the heart or the energy to start it up again.

But selling things was always, right from the beginning, a feature of Pilsdon life: milk was taken down every morning to the stand in churns; eggs were washed and crated and taken to the egg packing station near Crewkerne; Dorset blue Vinney cheese and cream cheeses were sold privately; vegetables, plants and sometimes home-made butter were also sold to visitors; pigs were fattened for collection by Walls; and Pilsdon boasted a pottery and later a craft room where all who came were free to buy whatever took their fancy.

The pottery was set up in one of the stone buildings behind the house. In the very early days the upstairs had been a bedroom and Percy, Ruth and I had used it as our bed-sitting room in the summer of 1959. Downstairs was the dairy and in the entrance to this we had racks for wellingtons and later one of our deep-freezers. But the upstairs was spacious and pleasant with a high-raftered roof and adjacent to it was a loft in which we stored apples and vegetables, and bottles and jars of every description. But it was in the bedroom area, which by then had been turned into a men's dormitory, that in 1966 pottery was begun. Bill, a highly skilled cabinet maker, who was staying with us, put up shelves round three sides of the room and built two pottery wheels; clay was ordered and, with the help and encouragement of Enid Haes and John Shelley, the pottery was launched and thereafter became a flourishing hobby and therapy. Later a teacher came over once a week from Weymouth, Patty Ellwood, and under her guidance and tuition many people learnt to 'throw a pot' at Pilsdon and some became very proficient, so much so that one man is now working full time on his own account making and teaching pottery. But it was not only mugs and vases and jugs that appeared on our shelves: the clay was also used for modelling and strange dragons, satyrs, dinosaurs, and creatures who looked as though they had stepped straight out of the pages of Tolkien appeared in various stages of making, pre-baking and glazing.

Later still, in 1976, the pottery was extended. Next to it was the apple loft which was approached by stone steps from the outside, the downstairs department of this construction being used as a coal hole. Fired by Miles's enthusiasm and knowledge of architecture, we knocked a large hole into the wall of the pottery thus giving internal access to the loft the inside of which was then transformed: partitions were removed, shelves and work tops constructed, and the rather dingy old barn became a clean and efficient craft room. We had an official Pilsdon opening for it and we had our first party there with coloured lights and pop corn and a mountain of delicious cheese dip. Subsequently this room was used for weaving and woodwork, enamelling, stone-polishing, painting, picture framing, leather work, and for displaying the pottery. And this was where we sold our crafts to any visitors who cared to buy them. Sometimes, in the summer, when big parties visited us once a week, it was difficult to keep the shelves supplied with a sufficient number of attractive wares. And this room became, in the evenings, a kind of den. Warmed by oil stoves, with the old rafters glowing in the light of candles and cushions generously thrown around the floor, more parties were held or people just sat and listened to music and chatted. An open-tread staircase led up from this room to a low-ceilinged loft where there was a lathe and some carpentry tools and up here, according to rumour, lived or at least walked, the Pilsdon ghost. Nobody ever went so far as to say they had actually seen anything but there were stories of footsteps which led nowhere and ended as mysteriously as they had begun. If you believe in ghosts then the old building was possibly haunted but if you are a sceptic then it is probably enough to know that the roof was rat-infested and that owls and bats and other night creatures were frequent visitors.

Because of the presence of the kiln there was mains electricity in the pottery and craft room and after all the house lights had been extinguished at 11 p.m. and the noisy generator had been silenced you could often see a gleam through the pottery windows as some late night worker plied his trade or an insomniac read his book or a secret assignation was kept. The only public long-player also lived up there so you might hear music floating down at any hour of the day or night.

But at Pilsdon we had chosen to identify ourselves with people's burdens and many problems found their way to us with which we had no technical knowledge or ability to deal. None of us had any psychiatric training and our doctor lived at Beaminster which was six miles away and, being a small and growing community, at first we accepted everyone who turned to us for help. Even in later years the doors of Pilsdon were always open day and night but the initial vision of helping all who came to us had to be modified when numbers increased to the point where not only was the house full with thirty to forty people but also requests for acceptance were pouring in by letter and telephone at the rate of five or six a day. But in 1960 when a fair-haired young man turned up one day at midnight and sat on the kitchen table swinging his plimsolled feet and explaining very apologetically why he had arrived so late and unannounced, he was welcomed in and no questions were asked.

Gradually experience taught us a great deal, most of all perhaps our limitations. But those early days were often chaotic. Life was then mostly movement from one crisis to another: drink was smuggled in; people's pills went missing; people went on walks and disappeared and had to be hunted for.

Various rumours circulated: that we were a mental hospital, a home for down-and-outs, an alcoholic hostel, and a nudist camp. This last was founded on nothing more than seeing a few Pilsdon men working out in the fields in summer stripped to the waist, but because the hedges were high and the lower half of the men could not be seen people presumed, such was our reputation, that they had no trousers on either.

On one occasion we had our Mini stolen. We were indulging in our usual cup of tea at eleven in the morning when Percy came in rather angrily saying that Evelyn knew perfectly well he wanted the car and why had she gone out in it. But at this point the innocent Evelyn was seen approaching the house across the lawn, whereupon we all realized that something was seriously wrong and we started a hunt for the Mini. It seemed so incredible that we found ourselves looking in the most impossible places where not even a child's toy car could have been hiding, much less the Mini. However we reluctantly came to the conclusion that, as not only the car but also one of our guests had disappeared, a most astonishing and open theft had taken place.

On another occasion Margaret, who was sleeping in a loose box outside the house, came to our bedroom in the early hours of the morning to say that she could hear strange noises coming from the direction of the garage. Percy and I crept downstairs. My heart was in my mouth. It was the only time at Pilsdon that I was really very frightened. Quietly we made our way round the courtyard to the garage. We found it empty but someone, and we could guess who, had smashed all the windows of the cars with a pick-axe. The pick-axe was lying discarded and the man was nowhere to be seen. I must confess that I was very glad not to have found him at work.

A valid question that might be asked here is how our daughter Ruth fared growing up as she did in the midst of all this. Later in the book she explains herself how she felt about it so I will only say here that, strangely enough, the incident that frightened her most was seeing a young girl have an epileptic fit at breakfast-time. It was not a bad fit but Ruth was sitting opposite her and so suffered the full shock of her loss of control. It frightened Ruth so much that she ran out of the house and was half-way up the hill before she was found and brought home again. But she was not at all frightened when two policemen brought a drunken man, shouting vociferously, into our bedroom in the middle of the night and, as our bedroom opened out of hers, it was her bedroom they came to first. It was a harmless enough incident as the man was merely trying in a misguided sort of way to stop the police from disturbing us at such an hour, but his protestations must have woken half the house.

The police were our friends and sometimes, when a new one came to our area he would pay us a social call. But sometimes they also found us uncooperative and difficult. I do not think they ever quite understood why, when they appeared on our doorstep with a drunken wayfarer whom they were unable to put in a cell for the night, we would tell them to take him away again. After all we seemed to exist to help such people so why did we refuse? And it was not always the police who found us obdurate: it might be a kindly stranger who had taken compassion on a benighted, homeless drunkard and found the same uncompromising strictness. Occasionally we were accused of being unchristian and much else besides, and if being a Christian means a constant milk and water kindness towards any and every action then we were undoubtedly, on occasions, unchristian. But Percy certainly thought Christianity was made of sterner stuff and so we preserved a strict rule about alcohol which served us well over the years and helped to give Pilsdon that security which so many of its guests desperately needed.

In the midst then of all these problems we struggled to help when and where we could often becoming over-involved ourselves in the emotional traumas of our guests while, at the same time, we were engaged in what sometimes seemed almost like a life and death battle to establish some kind of working harmony amongst ourselves. Perhaps we were not helped in this by the lack of privacy which was a marked feature of our life together. Percy and I shared a single bed-sitting room in the attics and the other community members nearly all had rooms to themselves but they were very small and, for most of the twenty years of which I am writing, they had no extra amenities such as an electric or gas fire, no power point or any facility for making themselves a private cup of tea or coffee. In winter it was impossible to use them as sitting-rooms at all unless you sat wrapped up in a rug with a hot-water bottle across your knees. So the communal rooms were used by us all and privacy was reduced to a minimum. Later we did have oil-fired central heating and it was then possible to retire to our own rooms and shut the door and be alone. Some of us needed this more than others but it was a need which grew on us all as the years went by so that, in some ways, the early days of sharing were friendlier and more generous. Although our proximity to each other exposed our tensions and disagreements and although the life was astringent almost to the point of harshness we were also warmed at the hearth of each other's care and friendship.

## V

"John next to Evelyn; Donald next to Anne; Mary next to me; Bill on the end; Walter next to Margaret," and so on until we were all, including the youngest, standing at our places behind our chairs in the dining-room waiting for grace to be said before we sat down to the meal.

Pilsdon was settling down.

But there are many pitfalls in the running of a community, especially when it is an unconventional one with no traditions behind it. Many do not survive the initial hazards. they run into financial trouble, or an attempt to be wholly democratic causes indecision and confusion, or they are unable to resolve their personality clashes and tensions. So, already, by about 1966, Pilsdon had been in existence longer than anyone had even dared to hope and had a full complement of thirty people. Gradually it was growing and taking shape.

The nucleus of the community was, by then, nine full members and these had the biggest responsibility for the care of the house and all who lived in it. They were Percy, Gillian, Uncle, Ethel, Margaret, Sidney, Evelyn, Anne, and myself. In addition there were always about twenty guests who stayed with us for shorter or longer periods. Most of them, but not all, were carrying a burden which was too heavy for them to cope with alone: alcoholism, drug addiction, acute loneliness, depression, marital breakdown, concealed homosexuality, nervous exhustion, mental illness, family pressure, social pressure, work pressure, a prison record, and just general inadequacy. These 'guests' were often brought to us by their families or friends, by welfare workers, doctors, or clergymen, and they came from every conceivable kind of home and background. They stayed with us, on average, about four months, some staying much longer, perhaps as much as four or five years, some only staying a few weeks or even days, and some took one look at us and went home, voluntarily or involuntarily, by the next train like the rather haughty lady whom we afterwards christened the Duchess.

She arrived one evening and reacted immediately against our slightly casual ways. There was no standing on ceremony at Pilsdon: you were called by your Christian name as soon as you came, indeed it was a sign of great intimacy to know anyone's surname. When you arrived you came into the kitchen for a cup of tea, and conversation with the hard-working cook might be desultory or even non-existent. This hardly suited the Duchess's ideas of how she should be treated and next morning at breakfast, having been given her work assignment for the day by Percy, she was so incensed by our life-style that she threw her cup of coffee at him and it landed on the immaculate fawn waistcoat of a man who was staying with us. It surprised no one that the Duchess was very soon enjoying the hospitality of the British Rail on a train that was bound for London.

Some of our guests stayed with us very much longer than the others and became firmly entrenched in the life of the community so that Pilsdon was for them, as for the full community members, both their home and their occupation. In one sense their position was slightly invidious as they were given, or acquired, a measure of responsibility not always acceded to the shorter term guests, but neither were they permanent community members so that their presence did sometimes tend to underline a hierarchical structure which we always hoped was only very lightly etched into our life. However, the community as a whole did rely fairly heavily on their supportive loyalty. It gave to the house an added feeling of stability and a sense of continuous tradition which became one of its strongest assets.

People sometimes referred to the permanent community members as the staff of Pilsdon but we never used this word partly because of its institutional overtones and partly because, being a religious community, we were not paid for the work we did or the service that we gave. We took no vows and there was no obligation to hand over all our money and possessions to the community but most of us had little that we could call our own. Percy and I had spent everything we had buying the house and had brought to it all our furniture and possessions, and may of the other members had sold their houses, and all gave up their cars for community use. So we received pocket-money from the community funds, and those who could supplemented it with what small income they might have, and one or two actually gave financial assistance to the house receiving none in return. Those of us who were the recipients of pocket-money were given an extra allowance for holidays and for pressing personal needs. There was no other security in financial terms, but that was the way we wanted it to be and that was the way it was for twenty years. But we were well provided for materially: we had a beautiful home, a sound roof over our heads, and a plentiful supply of our own home-grown food; we had community cars at our disposal, a library of books, and the generosity of all our friends.

The people who stayed with us were very often on social security and of this we were given the lion's share while the rest was their own and was used mainly for tobacco and sweets which we sold at our own little shop. Later the money had to stretch to jars of Nescafé and tea bags when we had instituted an electric kettle in the bootroom where anyone could brew themselves a mug of tea or coffee. Those of our guests who had private means also paid to stay with us but we had no absolute fixed fee: Pilsdon was never a place to which people could not afford to come. This then, together with the sale of milk and eggs, fattened pigs, cheese, garden produce and pottery was our only regular source of income, supplemented always by the generous gifts of friends, and a few legacies. No grants or salaries came from anywhere: Percy was never paid for his services to the church and was not, technically, its vicar although in practice he took nearly all the services. In 1970 Pilsdon became a charitable trust and deeds of covenant helped the financial situation but even then we remained an entirely independent, voluntary body and we ourselves were the trustees.

But the support of people's friendship was a great wealth. We had hardly started living at Pilsdon when students came from Westcott House in Cambridge to help with anything that was needed and other students gave up vacation and holiday time to join in with everything that was going on. Rotarians from Lyme Regis came regularly in 1959 to help with the laying of floors in the loose boxes that we converted into bedrooms. Bunny and Norman Fairchild came every day for many years to work in both the flower and vegetable gardens and Sylvia Perham came from Axminster to do the same. It would be impossible, and perhaps undesirable, to mention the names of all our helpers but they were legion. They gave us so much that we needed in terms of material, emotional and spiritual support, and we, in our turn, gave to their lives I think the meaningfulness, the colour and variety and vigour engendered by community living.

Clothing for us and for our guests was never a problem. The clothes cupboard featured largely in our communal life. People's generosity made it possible for us to have a large store of second-hand clothing and out of this stock we were able to provide for those of our guests who came to us with only what they stood up in. And we ourselves could nearly always find what we needed. After 1965, when Anne joined us this store came to be known as Anne's Boutique. Anne was in charge of it and I never ceased to marvel at her incredible ability to find just exactly the right thing for everybody. Sometimes when Anne was away I would go rummaging around in the boutique for a shirt or trousers or jacket and not only did it take me twice as long as Anne to find what I was looking for but also the unfortunate man I was trying to help generally ended up looking like Charlie Chaplin.

Sometimes the clothes we received were of very high quality. One wayfarer became the proud possessor of a Hardy Amies jacket and I had a Dior suit handed to me by Anne that I went on stuffing myself into long after it had grown too small for me. Of course we bought some of our clothes as well and gave them to each other for Christmas and birthday presents. There was nothing uniform or drab about the way we dressed. Our young people were mostly as trendy as young people anywhere else. When skirts went up we shortened ours and wore them above our knees, and when they came down again we added frills and lace. We had a Laura Ashley craze and all went about in long skirts sprinkled with tiny flowers and frills around our necks. When silver was in we wore silver bracelets and rings and when gold was in we wore narrow gold chains. Our clothes were not perhaps the latest word in urban elegance — country life is more suited to wellingtons than winkle-pickers — but we followed in the wake of current fashions and if they were too expensive we made them ourselves.

Not only were we given clothes for the boutique but almost everything else as well. Furniture was regularly offered to us and crockery, sheets and pillowcases, blankets and towels although we did occasionally go to sales and acquire some bargains. From one sale Gillian came back with a pile of towels. They were white and had a broad blue band down the middle bearing the caption Cunard White Star Line. We used them for many years. They were patched and repatched and one night Gillian dreamt she was getting married and the veil over her head was a white towel inscribed with the words Cunard White Star Line. Books were given to the library, cooking equipment to the kitchen, washing machines to the laundry, a full sized billiard table, television sets, cows, pigs, bees, and a beautiful zinc water butt with the date 1712 which stood against the back wall of the house and looked as though it had grown there.

Life by 1966 had also achieved a framework of orderliness. The day to day routine was established and changed very little over the years. The morning started for most people with a bell at 7.25 followed almost immediately by morning prayers in the chapel. This small chapel was inside the house but services were entirely voluntary. Pilsdon was not overtly religious: you could believe in anything or nothing and still be welcome as a guest of the community. Whether your bible was *The Lord of the Rings*, or Shakespeare, or *Das Kapital*, or the *Bhagavadgita* you could stay at Pilsdon and propound your theories to anyone who would listen and in the kitchen, especially in the evening over a cup of tea or cocoa, conversation flowed freely.

After the morning service which was a short form of Matins followed by Holy Communion there was breakfast at 8 and for most people the 7.25 bell was the preliminary to this. Porridge, corn flakes, home-made muesli, yoghourt, poached or fried eggs or bacon, toast and marmalade, and tea or coffee were quickly disposed of and if you were too comfortably tucked under the bedclothes and arrived in the dining-room at 8.25 you might find nothing left but half a piece of cold toast, and brave indeed was the guest who expected breakfast in bed.

At breakfast we all used the dining-room but we sat wherever we liked and came and went according to the dictates of our stomachs so the meal was relatively informal. But it was at breakfast-time that Percy gave out the work schedule for the day. Some people's jobs were fixed for a few weeks or even months but others, especially those who were new to Pilsdon, had to be given a daily task. It surprised many people to learn that men and women not only paid to stay at the community but were also expected to do a reasonable day's work. And it was also surprising how readily most people accepted this. Percy believed very strongly in the therapy of work and most of us, even when we are on holiday, like to have something to do and are the better for it. Certainly it helped men and women to forget their troubles for a while and get things into slightly better perspective. Pilsdon never encouraged getting together into huddles brooding over ailments and we were also saved from some of this by the fact that very few people shared the same troubles. The diversity of problems was one of the unique features of Pilsdon. However it was difficult, especially in winter, to find work for everyone and often our inventiveness was sorely taxed as we rummaged in our minds for some floor somewhere that might possibly need scrubbing or a hedge that might need to be trimmed. When you have a large old manor house, a big vegetable and fruit garden, an orchard, flower beds and cutting garden, a couple of fields, hedges, ditches, drains, a reservoir, cows, pigs and chickens, there are a multitude of things that need doing but some of the jobs need specialized care and knowledge and strength so that not everyone could be slotted into just any available work space. However something was always found for everyone and, if necessary, overalls, wellington boots and dungarees as well.

After the meals the washing-up was done in pairs. We had no machine for this and at each meal Percy would turn cheerfully to two luckless people with the remark, "Would you like to make friends over the sink?" Perhaps a few people did but it was just as easy to make enemies that way. It was not uncommon for voices to be raised in anger in the washing-up pantry and on occasions someone could be heard storming out of the room. There seem to be so many fads and whims connected with washing-up. We belonged to the two-sink brigade, one sink for washing and one for rinsing, but some people are fast and casual, others slow and conscientious; some washers do not mind having their dirty forks returned to them while others take it as a personal insult and object furiously, and some driers are so slow that there is very soon no available space left on the draining-board. Sometimes one of the pair would sit down comfortably to a cup of coffee after supper and forget all about the assignation at the sink until, perhaps reminded of it by someone or something, he would hurry away to the pantry only to be greeted by a partner purple in the face with steam and anger spitting out, "It's all finished now anyway!" Many people would have preferred to do the whole job themselves but Percy always insisted on team work. For many years he did the washing-up himself with someone every Saturday evening and everyone in the house except the cooks was called on regularly.

There was a break at eleven for a cup of tea and biscuits and a visit to the shop. We had our own small shop which supplied most of the immediate necessities of life such as tobacco and sweets, toothbrushes and toothpaste, writing materials, shampoo, razor blades, birthday cards, fruit juices, and tights. Later, when there was an electric kettle for general use, the shop did a flourishing trade in Nescafé and Tetley tea bags. A few times we had trouble with people picking the lock and trying to wrench the door open but we seldom kept much money inside.

Lunch was at about five or ten past one depending on the cook's punctuality or lack of it, and it was preceded by another short service in the chapel when prayers took a more informal turn and there was opportunity for quiet thought and meditation. This chapel was very small and separated a little from the hustle and bustle of the rest of the house. It had been used as an office by the previous owners but it was beautifully panelled from ceiling to floor and when we started using it as a chapel it was still further enhanced by the addition of deep blue velvet curtains. There was a simple cross and candle-sticks on one windowsill and a statuette of St Francis on the other, and in one corner a tall wrought-iron container in which there were always flowers. And here people used to come to read, to pray, to meditate, to think, just to be quiet. It was a tiny room but much of the strength and purpose of Pilsdon emanated from its stillness.

Lunch, like supper, was more formal except in the summer when we often had it outside on the lawn. Percy gave people their places as they came in to the dining-room and we waited, standing, until grace had been said. This was a procedure new to many people and some embarrassment was caused by people finding themselves sitting down with everyone standing up around them. The cook of the week served the food from a large dresser and it was taken round by anyone who offered assistance. It was generally thick soup, or a cheese or egg or vegetable dish, followed by home-made bread and butter, jam, Cheddar cheese and Pilsdon cream cheese with herbs and garlic or apricots and walnuts, and sometimes there would be a bowl of apples.

We sat down to the meal together under the stern gaze of Mr and Mrs Ferrar, the mother and father of Nicholas Ferrar of Little Gidding. They were large portraits painted in the seventeenth century, the only copies of the originals which are at Cambridge, and they were given to the community by a member of the Ferrar families. Percy himself sat at the head of the main table and I sat at the foot, the community members all had their special places and everyone else sat at a different place each time. Putting people round at lunch and again at supper was a job I hated doing when Percy was away from home. I knew I ought to mix people up indiscriminately but wanted them to enjoy their meal without personality clashes so that I found it difficult to make snap decisions as people filed into the room. And sometimes, if guests arrived late, I might have forgotten about them and they then had to be squeezed into any available space. When we were very full there would also have to be a few people eating in the kitchen though we generally managed to crowd into the dining-room together.

It was at lunch that we entertained most of the visitors who were not staying at the house, partly so that they could be shown round in the daytime but, as we had our dinner at night, it was sometimes necessary to warn them that the soup was not the prelude to a three-course meal otherwise a slightly strained look slowly spread over their features as they allowed their soup plate to be removed and then suddenly realized they had no fork and that hopes of a second helping of soup were fast vanishing in the direction of the washing-up pantry. On one occasion we were entertaining the Prince and Princess of Rumania who were at that time living near us. In the morning Gill, who was cook that week, asked me whether I thought spaghetti bolognese might be suitable for the lunch-time menu and I, reflecting vaguely that spaghetti was a continental speciality, assured her that it would do splendidly. However when the meal arrived I found myself sitting next to the Prince. He was managing his spaghetti beautifully, rolling it around his fork like a true connoisseur but every time he turned to speak to me I had long strands of it hanging out of my mouth and the clipping of them off with my teeth precluded any very intelligent replies and I cursed myself for so airily agreeing to Gill's suggestion.

After lunch work was supposed to be resumed at 2.15 and continued until the tea bell went at 4.30. Sometimes it would be someone's birthday tea and we very early started to celebrate them. These were one of the more light-hearted features of Pilsdon life. We cajoled people into telling us when their birthdays were and for many years kept a list of them all on a calendar hanging up in the kitchen. However publicity did not appeal to everyone. Shy people were sometimes terrified of the approach of their birthdays and one or two wayfarers actually left just before the arrival of the dreaded day. But on the whole people were pleased to have their birthdays remembered and many confessed to never having had a birthday cake before. When it was a child's birthday we also had ice-cream and jelly and chocolate biscuits and balloons and small presents for all the other invited children. These were generally neighbours and sometimes school friends of the Pilsdon boy or girl. Some of the mothers would help with the cake and party but it was a daunting prospect for anyone who was a little shy or lacking in self-confidence and many of the mothers were only too pleased to sit back and let us get on with it.

After tea was over work for most people was finished except in the summer when, if it was very hot, we sometimes worked after tea instead of after lunch and there might be haymaking again after supper. Evensong was at 6.30 and supper at 7. This was our main meal and consisted of the usual meat with two vegetables and a pudding, and it was followed by coffee served in the common room, and occasionally chocolates which visiting friends had brought. Some people stayed on then especially when it was cold and there was a big log fire blazing on the hearth and we talked and read and knitted, and slept curled up in the big comfortable chairs.

We did eventually possess two television sets and these were watched assiduously in the evening. They were housed in two separate rooms outside the main building and each was sacred to its own rites. By this method argument was virtually eliminated. If you wanted to watch BBC 1 you went to an old stone-built outhouse which we had converted into a recreation room and which also held a full-sized billiard table. And if you wanted BBC2 you went to a put-it-up-yourself wooden chalet which we had erected in a corner of the field at the back of the house. Both rooms were heated and boasted half a dozen or more comfortable old arm chairs, but the BBC2 room was the smarter, being new, and was much the warmer. The BBC1 room had a stone floor and stone walls. It was large and difficult to keep adequately heated, also it housed a family of mice one of which was always scuttling up and down the water pipes which went the whole length of the east wall, and it was used as a doss house for our one-night-stay wayfarers – and rumour had it that it sometimes housed other 'wee fellers' as well. Occasionally we also watched televistion during the day, the rigid protocol between the two rooms would be dropped and we all crowded into the BBC2 room to watch Wimbledon or the Olympics on BBC1. We ran our own sweepstake for the Grand National so the attendance was always high and most of us watched the boat race which we sadistically enjoyed most in 1978 when the Cambridge team sank. It spiced the event with real excitement.

We also had our own home-made amusements in the evenings. For several years there was an enthusiastic group who did Scottish dancing every Wednesday, and friends came in from outside Pilsdon to teach, support and encourage. The biggest snag, as with most things we did was that, as newcomers were constantly joining the group, it was difficult for the more proficient to feel any progress was being made. This was true also of the choir which met every Friday evening but as the activities of the choir spanned the whole twenty years of which I am writing and as some people belonged to it for the whole of that time, and as it also had to perform regularly in public, the choir did slowly but rather unevenly acquire greater skill and musicality.

Our other recreations were snooker and billiards, table tennis, darts, and a host of indoor games of which the favourite was always Scrabble though we also played Chinese chequers, draughts, backgammon, Monopoly, chess, solitaire, Cluedo, card games and, almost feverishly one winter, table skittles. We were always given a selection of indoor games for Christmas and one of them always tended to take preference over the others. But most of these were winter pastimes. On summer evenings we lazed outside on the lawn chatting, or went for late swims, and we sometimes unearthed from the summerhouse an old croquet set and although none of us knew how to play properly and the rule book was missing we wielded the mallets with great enthusiasm. Bowls too sped on their way across the front lawn. So we amused ourselves as, deep in the heart of the country, you have to do.

The last rites of the day were the evening service of Compline at 9.10 and a cup of tea or cocoa in the kitchen at 9.30. Sometimes, if you were lucky, this might be brought out to you on a tray to the television room. Some of the men were adept at handling a tray piled high with mugs in one hand while opening a series of doors with the other though, on windy days, this delicate operation was fraught with hazards as the path outside the kitchen door was a funnel for every lightest breeze and a strong gust could whip the cocoa right out of the cups before you had taken three steps. Later, at 11, the generator was silenced, the lights extinguished and, at least in theory, people went to bed and to sleep.

So a pattern of life emerged and for most people it was a healthy, happy tonic concocted of fresh air, fresh food, tired muscles, friendship, and an overall feeling of being a useful member of a relatively harmonious team. This was primarily what Pilsdon offered to the many hundreds who, over twenty years, stayed there as its guests, and it was a small minority who tasted it only once and did not come back for more.

This pattern was further assisted by a framework of orderliness and discipline at Pilsdon and the thread of firm authority which stemmed from Percy's direction and which underpinned the whole fabric of our life was nowhere more clearly visible than in the relative formality of lunch and supper. Everybody was expected to be there unless they were ill or had informed the cook they were going out, or wanted urgently to watch a programme on television which clashed with the time of the meal, or had embarked on a very necessary crash slimming campaign. But this formal setting was a painful trial to some of our guests. Many found it difficult to sit right through a meal and even washing-up was a happy release as it could be started before the meal was over. Shy, nervous people liked to be placed as near the doors as possible and for them the most dreaded position in the room was against the wall at the long table from which place there was no possibility of escape until the meal was over and we had all been freed at a sign from Percy. Perhaps formal meals could have been eliminated but they were the only times when we were all together and they gave a necessary structure to the community life which could probably not have been achieved in any more congenial way.

The discipline exercised by Percy over the life of the community was probably the strongest single factor in its survival kit. He gradually learnt how to tell the distinguishing signs of mental illness or emotional unbalance and was very often able to gauge fairly accurately who could be helped by a stay at Pilsdon and who was too disturbed to benefit from it. And sometimes he had to exert what seemed like a ruthless authority in turning out from the community men and women who were threatening to wreck the peace and harmony and stability of the whole. This was usually his own decision and it was a heavy burden to carry and gave him sometimes a harshness of temper and stern impatience which belied his real concern. Fortunately it did not have to happen very often but the possibility was always there and, with it, the potential for making a wrong decision. All this Percy chose to bear alone and his autocratic methods did not win universal approval. Patriarchal authority is highly suspect now when even paternalism is a questionable value and many people who came to Pilsdon or heard of it had very different views on organization and control. There is no doubt at all that Pilsdon was not structured democratically: we never had meetings of the whole community and only fairly infrequent and irregular meetings for the permanent members. There were certain areas of work for which we did assume the responsibility but they were only parts of the total system and that system itself was under Percy's direct authority. It was he who decided who should come and, if necessary, who should go, and it was he who organized, and indeed galvanized, the day's activities.

This did tend to lessen the opportunities for individual responsibility but it also gave to Pilsdon a firm basis so that people who felt insecure or inadequate could live and work there without undue fear or worry. Many people were suffering from acute anxiety and it was considerably diminished by the knowledge of a strong leadership. All this was especially true of the early years. Later, when the traditions of Pilsdon were well established and respected, Percy was able to loosen the control a little and it is possible that by now the community may be able to move into an area where a more democratic organization can operate within an acknowledged leadership. However, over the twenty years of which I am writing everybody at Pilsdon felt the unequivocal directness of Percy's authority and many leaned heavily upon it and it contributed much to their well-being.

But within this overall control there was undoubtedly an area of great freedom at Pilsdon. You could wear your hair long or short without comment — and those were the days when long hair for men was frowned on by traditionalists; you could wear shoes or go barefoot, and one young man who stayed with us never wore any at all, not even when he was working in the hay stubble, until he had to go to a wedding and appeared in a wonderful pair of long hide boots. You could strum away on your guitar and find an appreciative audience; you could sketch or paint without arousing mockery; you could be silent without remonstrance or talk if you felt like it, and you could be politically red or blue or pink or a neutral white. There were only two things you could not do and by and large these two rules were honoured more in the observance than in the breach. You could not imbibe alcohol either at the house or at the local pub, and you could not refuse to work. We only had one guest who ever stayed at the house and consistently refused his allotted task and got away with it. Gavin was a mongoloid boy who stayed at Pilsdon for his holidays over a period of about four years and won a secure place in the affections of the whole community. And it was only Gavin who dared to say, when Percy was giving out jobs at breakfast-time, "No. Gavin no weed paths. Percy weed paths," and the refusal was laughingly accepted.

The denial of alcohol was not because the community as such was teetotal — indeed it was a hardship to many community members to have to forgo it — but because it was more helpful to the alcoholics who stayed with us if everyone was involved in the same abstinence. And the work was obligatory not because people paid nothing to stay with us — they both paid and worked — but because, when thirty people live together as we did, the communal life depends upon everyone pulling their weight and handling their share of the multitudinous jobs needing to be done. Also Percy believed very strongly in the therapy of work although the work was done neither for money nor to further any private ambition: it was done as a form of service to the community, and most communities exist to learn and practise this kind of service as against purely private gain. It was largely this which helped to re-create in many people a social sense and a social loyalty which had either been spoilt or stunted by an unfortunate start in life or by later experiences of rejection.

We were often asked what our aim was at Pilsdon and it was never easy to give a simple answer. Ernest Bevin is reported to have said, 'I am not a very strong believer in Constitutions. I like the thing that grows, the thing that evolves.' He would perhaps have approved of Pilsdon. It was like a spider spinning its web out of its own body. However, we are listed as a religious community and all communities have certain elements in common: they all provide support and friendship and lessen the burden of isolation especially for single people, unmarried, widowed, or divorced, and they all provide an opportunity to mix with people of all ages and from widely differing backgrounds. It is especially noticeable that they lessen the generation gap because old and young are sharing in something together and working towards the same end.

All communities too are distinct from institutions. Although people live together in schools, hospitals, prisons, and hostels of all kinds, these are institutions rather than communities. They are organized and run by a paid staff for the benefit of people who need, or are relegated to, their services. There is generally a strong line of demarcation between the staff and the patients, pupils, prisoners, or other recipients of whatever the institution offers, and they have little or no option about being there. Whereas, in a community, although there may be some form of hierarchy, an organized existence and an acceptance of leadership, the choice of whether or not to live there is voluntary, there is no paid staff, and each person involved with that community is concerned with the building up and strengthening of the community life by service to it and by a sense of care and responsibility for all its members. And so it was to preserve Pilsdon as a community that, although we did accept people who were referred to us by social welfare workers for rehabilitation, they had to want to come themselves and say so. Percy always insisted on this and he consistently refused to have anyone at Pilsdon as a result of a court order making it a condition of residence. It had to be an open-ended transaction. People had to be free to come and free to go. And it also greatly increased our sense of community that we all worked together, existed on much the same amount of pocket-money, and lived as one large family, so that we had a feeling of oneness which is scarcely possible in even a liberal and kindly institution.

But although a community is not an institution and all communities have things in common which set them apart from the more normal pattern of life in the world, each community also has its own distinctive purpose and style of living. So now I will, very briefly, outline the objectives or basic characteristics of some well-established communities with which we had some contact at Pilsdon and show how we differed from them, and I hope they will forgive me if extreme brevity makes for inaccuracy in describing them.

Near us, in West Dorset, was the Anglican Franciscan Friary known to most people as Cerne Abbas although it is some distance from the town of Cerne itself. The Friary is part of a traditional monastic order with its vows, its system of novices and its eventual lifelong commitment: but we took no vows, had no novitiate, and were not committed to Pilsdon for the rest of our lives, nor had we given up all our personal possessions. Not far away, on the north coast of Devon, was the community of Lee Abbey, a huge conference centre and evangelistic spearhead for the Church of England: but we did not hold confernces and our religious views were divergent or non-existent. We also had some contact with the Richmond Fellowship which has an increasing number of houses to provide a supportive background for men and women who have had a mental breakdown and have returned to normal or semi-normal employment: but our concern was not exclusively with the mentally sick nor did we continue to provide a home for people after they had returned to work. We had a little contact with the healing home at Burrswood: but we were not a place set apart for healing even though a form of healing did sometimes occur. And we were not a hostel on the lines of the Simon communities for those shipwrecked by drink, or the Langley Houses for ex-prisoners. Up on the exposed east coast of Scotland, near Elgin, is the Findhorn Community, now a university of light, a college to educate men and women in the thought and vision and aspirations of the new Aquarian age: but we were not concerned with an educational process, neither were we programmed to a special kind of belief. We were not a commune like the small groups which have come into existence in many urban centres to combat the loneliness and anonymity of town life. And neither were we a community on the lines of the kibbutzim in Israel. In *The Children of the Dream* which is about the first generation of children reared in kibbutz, Bruno Bettelheim concurs with the view of Stanley Diamond that the kibbutz is not an extended family and this, in one sense, is exactly what we were.

We were a family, a large extended family of men, women, and children which had thrown its doors wide open to the questing, the doubting, the troubled, the homeless, the helpless, the unwanted, the unloving and the unloved. We had a patriarchal family structure: meals were family meals with all of us gathered together in one dining-room; prayers were family prayers, however many or few cared to attend; and in a large family there is always plenty of work for everyone especially if that family lives in the country and runs a small farm, and everyone in a family is expected to help with the work. There was family affection between us and there were also family rows: there were strong bonds of loyalty and also the irritations of too much proximity. But one family feature was noticeably lacking — there was no family likeness between us. Rather we must have been the most heterogeneous collection of people ever to be gathered under one roof. This was perhaps the single most distinctive thing about Pilsdon. We were a very mixed bag and this gave our life a healthy variety and breadth which drew people into its orbit and brought them back time and time again.

This is how one young man expressed this family spirit:

I first came to Pilsdon on a cold wet spring day in 1975. My first impression was all this is too good to be true, "there has got to be a catch". It took me quite a long time to realize that there was no catch and that the only trap was one of love. It is very hard to be given love day in day out and not return it. When I first came, it was straight from H.M. prison Pentonville and the contrast from a stark and dirty prison to a place of such love and light may well have helped me to see Pilsdon through rose-tinted glasses, but it is a vision that has never left me and I doubt that it ever will.

I don't say Pilsdon is an easy place to live, at times it can be very hard and demanding. In a way we of Pilsdon are a very large family with one big home. So like any family home there are always conflicts and irritations, but the difference here is that conflicts are soon sorted out and forgotten bringing people closer together and not further apart.

To me Pilsdon is a home, a family, a place of refuge when there is no where else I feel I can turn and go. I know I can always come back to Pilsdon heal my wounds and go back to the world stronger and ready to try and pick up the pieces.

## VI

Pilsdon quickly began to have a distinct 'feel' of its own and to give you some idea of that feel perhaps the best place to take you would be the kitchen. This is where you would find yourself if you had just arrived. It is a farmhouse kitchen full of the smells of fresh dough, and home-made jam and pickles, with the occasional weak little runt squealing in a box beside the Aga and, just outside, the dairy with milk from our own cows standing in great pans.

The kitchen hummed and throbbed with the news and activities of the whole community. It was not only a kitchen but an entrance hall, a waiting-room, a clinic, a dispensary, a sitting-room, a sorting office, and a nursery. It was small wonder that the cook was often nearly distraught and yet had to try and keep her cool while the lazy sat on the kitchen chairs, the cold sat on the Aga rail, babies and small children sat on the table, and night-cap addicts sat absolutely everywhere. In these circumstances the Pilsdon cook of the week provided nourishing meals for thirty, baked bread, made cakes and biscuits for visiting parties, stirred about three hundred pounds of marmalade and probably the same amount of jam, pickled, bottled, and prepared fruit and vegetables for one, then two, and later three deep freezers, and coped with a head suddenly appearing round the door at 12.30 announcing with studied casualness "Oh. Sorry. Didn't anyone tell you? My sister and her husband and three kids are all coming to lunch today. I do hope it's all right."

This then was the Pilsdon kitchen, the warm heart of the house and the symbol of its country family feel. We all knew it could have been otherwise: the door could have been shut to all intruders; smokers could have been thrown out; some other room could have been set aside for the reception of visitors, and it was not absolutely imperative that the first-aid kit be kept on the kitchen shelf. But this is how it was and this is how we wanted it to be. Pilsdon was a family home, not an institution, and in a large family this is what the kitchen usually becomes. Mum is there and so, gradually, is everything else.

Not that Mum was always the same person. For many years she was either Gillian or myself. We took it in turns to cook, and cooked for a week with one day off somewhere in the middle. Sunday could never be a day off for the Pilsdon cook. On that day there was a roast lunch to be prepared and served up and supper provided for everyone who came to Evensong in the little church. In the winter this might only be an extra twenty or thirty unless snow lay deep on the ground, in which case there might be no one from outside at all. But in summer this meant making salad or pizza — Gillian's speciality — and bread and cakes for about eighty or ninety people. Of course the work was not all done on the Sunday itself: the freezer was often groaning with bread and cake. But still, when Sunday came there always seemed to be plenty to do not only for the cook but also for the unfortunate person chosen to do dining-room duty on that day.

Nobody liked this job. The usual dining-room 'king' or 'queen' (our word for the person in charge of any operation) had a holiday on Sunday so some other poor volunteer always had to be conscripted for the job. Sometimes it would be a visitor new to Pilsdon with only the haziest notion of what happened or where everything was kept. And of course the routine was different on that day from any other so that if it was a novice on duty the cook sometimes needed more than her usual self-control not to throw around the kitchen something more than a mere tantrum. And if, as sometimes happened, the same person found himself or herself doing dining-room duty on Sundays for weeks or even months on end the air in the rear regions of the house turned blue.

But on quiet days when the house was not too full and Christmas and Easter were both distant dreams, the kitchen was a very pleasant place. In winter it was warm when everywhere else was cold. There was an Aga already installed in the house when we bought it and this was the pride and joy of our lives. It never went out unless you were guilty of the most gross neglect.

In the early days of Pilsdon when I was a domestic greenhorn, this happened to me several times until the routine disciplines of life in community had taken the fine edge off my absent-mindedness. The process of resuscitation in itself was enough to lessen the dangers of forgetfulness. It involved getting down on your hands and knees with your face nearly in the ashes and poking tiny bits of firelighter in through the grating at the bottom and, as half the firelighter generally fell out again, it took a very long time before the coals started to show red once more. As my lapses always seemed to find me out at ten to eleven at night I was often sitting up nursing the sick Aga until one or two in the morning. I was warm enough but the house was very large and very dark and silent and I sometimes hardly dared to look around. No one had ever actually seen a ghost at Pilsdon but you never knew — the house was nearly four hundred years old and many people's memories must have been haunting its stone walls and cavities.

Perhaps the best kitchen time used to be nine o'clock at night. Work was done for the day and here everybody congregated for a final cup of tea or cocoa before bedtime. Sometimes every chair and table-top was occupied and often the floor space too and discussions on every conceivable topic went on until the early hours of the morning. Candles were officially frowned on as being a potential fire hazard but I think there were few nights when the twinkle of a candle did not glow dimly across the courtyard from the kitchen windows and when its soft light did not encourage the sharing of secret fears and desires.

During the day the kitchen was a hive of activity and none was better loved than butter-making. We had no churn so we did it, in the early days, by plunging our hands into the thick yellow cream and gently swishing it round and round until the buttery granules started to separate from the buttermilk — the curds and whey of Little Miss Muffet. As this sometimes took about two hours it was a tedious and tiring occupation and well-nigh impossibly time-consuming for the cook herself but there was never any shortage of willing helpers. Everybody loved causing the miraculous transformation and of course it did involve being allowed to sit in the lovely cosy kitchen for hours on end just doodling in a bowl of rich cream.

There was another, winter only, occupation which though less attractive became an absorbing passion with some people — the cutting up of thirty pounds of Seville oranges and converting them into marmalade. It is difficult to imagine this becoming an obsession but it certainly bit deep into the fanaticism of a few, just as slicing beans did later in the year. I was one of those bean-slicing addicts. Once I had begun I found it almost impossible to stop until the last tiny under-developed bean had been removed from the enormous thirty pound basket and salted and packed into the great glass bottles which looked like old-fashioned sweet jars. I always half expected to see them filled with gob stoppers and aniseed balls.

The bean-slicing, although technically a kitchen chore, was hardly ever done in the kitchen. A party of people would sally forth onto the grass at the back of the house armed with saucepans, dishes, and kitchen knives, and sit there in the sun chatting and slicing until the beans were done. It was not exactly a popular job in itself but it was companionable and everybody loved the fruits of the labour — cooked beans liberally sprinkled with chopped-up hard-boiled egg, or hot beans with chunks of potato and crispy bacon over which was thrown a French dressing with a little raw sliced onion.

The 'slim is healthy' campaign had not hit Pilsdon in its early days. That came later and, by now, the traditional four-thirty tea has been almost completely abolished. But for twenty years we had a happy and hearty belief in the old-fashioned institution of afternoon tea with sandwiches piled high and plenty of home-made cake and biscuits. In the winter we all gathered for this around the log fire in the sitting-room and for many people it was the favourite meal of the day, partly I think because of the informality of its setting. You could sit with your friends and with a bit of cunning and a small amount of sleight of hand nobody need know you had managed to consume six egg sandwiches, four large slices of cake, and a handful of flapjacks.

The tremendous tea was prepared in the kitchen by two different people each day. Percy had the slightly misguided idea that, like the washing-up, it might induce friendship. I do not think it was a very popular job, especially with the men, but at least in winter it brought you in out of the freezing garden for an hour in the afternoon. The cook had done the baking for it but the making of the sandwiches and the laying out of the cakes and biscuits was the responsibility of the tea-makers so the teas showed considerable individual talent and we once, accidentally, had cold gravy sandwiches. But no tea-maker was popular unless egg sandwiches appeared on the table — paste and marmite were poor and rather dry substitutes — and as we had our own chickens they hardly ever failed to be supplied.

Special birthday teas were very much a feature of our community life — and the cook's headache. A huge birthday cake had to be produced, sometimes at short notice as when we asked one girl when her birthday was and got the answer "Today". These cakes not only had to be big enough to go round thirty or more people, with second helpings if possible, but had to be decorated to suit the characteristics of the recipient. They taxed the cook's ingenuity to the utmost and used to take me all afternoon to create. In the early years they tended to be representational. Gill made me a masterpiece. It was the church harmonium — which I was then still doing battle with in the church — made out of chocolate sponge with tiny black and white keys, pedals, music, and even a minute bowl of flowers. I responded by endeavouring to make her a cow which, for obvious reasons, had to be lying down. But the head, which was made of a separate sponge cake, would keep falling off and eventually had to be stuck on with such a thick layer of icing that the neck looked more as though it belonged to a prize bull.

Later on, my skill and inspiration faded, and I took to composing little verses which I then piped on to the cake. This had the advantage that they could be thought up in bed the night before and so the actual process of decorating the cake was cut by half. And in due course Gill took to the practice so that doggerel became the order of the day for birthday cakes. Not long ago when I was turning out some drawers I came across a notebook containing some of these birthday rhymes and I include them here because they show something of the mixture of fun and affection which was so big a part of our life.

There was:

> When you are in trouble or in dire distress
> Just give a shout for Walter and he will do the rest;
> If it's soot inside your chimney or the lore of any game,
> Or an acrobat for parties, Walter is the name.

and a playful dig in:
> Has anybody seen my specs?
> I had them here just a minute ago
> And now I can't think what I've done with them so,
> Do please just say if you saw them go.
> Hasn't anybody seen my specs?

this for a beach enthusiast:
> I must go down to the sea again, to the summer sea and the sky,
> And all I ask is a swim suit and a towel to dry me by,
> And the old grey van, and a salty tang, and a merry, laughing driver,
> And back to a bumper Pilsdon tea when the long cool swim is over.

and how I managed to get the whole of the next one onto one cake now beats my imagination:
> In the Pilsdon tribe there was once a man
> Whose surname was Byrne and his Christian name Dan.
> By his brogue you could tell he had sojourned a while
> And been born on the shores of the Emerald Isle.
> With gutters and slates he was quite a dab hand,
> Fifty foot high on a roof he could stand.
> The winter he scorned and despite ice and snow
> A buttonless shirt displayed half his torso.
> For lightness of foot he could outdo a score,
> At a waltz or Paul Jones he was first on the floor.
> In the magistrate's court he help would have none,
> His innocence clear, he would stand all alone.
> Fine tales I could tell but of space I'm bereft,
> A wee bit of cake is all that is left,
> So here's to the birthday of this gallant man
> Best known to the world as Pilsdon Dan.

The cook was always helped in the kitchen by one other regular person and a few irregular ones. The latter were generally people staying at Pilsdon for a shortish period and for whom no long-term occupation had been found. Or perhaps they might be lonely people who needed company while they worked or people who were not strong enough to do manual work in the garden, disabled people possibly or people with bad backs or weak hearts. This was an operation which could have been described as helping the helper and I was not very good at it. I found it confusing and was not sufficiently sure of myself in the kitchen to enjoy being watched while working or to be able to delegate responsibility with ease. In this area my own sensitivity often precluded sufficient sensitivity to the needs of other people.

The regular helper was usually a trained kitchen porter, a man accustomed to working in hotel kitchens. He was what we called a 'cowboy'. Very probably he would be Scottish or Irish and he would find himself drying out after a spell on the roads in the Pilsdon kitchen. As kitchen porters –

KPs — the cowboys ran the whole gamut of capability or lack of it. A good KP was heaven-sent but a bad KP was an unqualified disaster. On the whole the cooks and KPs worked well together though I do remember to my shame rounding furiously on one unfortunate man who had just arrived to help me and who seemed to be presumptuously trying to run the kitchen for me. But many of them became our close friends though we never knew when they were going to take off and disappear even if the potatoes were half peeled, and dirty dishes piled mountain high. The call of the wild was generally the call of alcohol. Many of them fought hard against this but without a home or family or tie or responsibility in the world resistance was on very slippery ground.

The kitchen had a beautiful flagstone floor which was easier to keep clean than most of the imitation tiles and vinyls. Every day this floor was washed down, the more energetic KPs scrubbing it on hands and knees and, in the early days especially, this was a necessary routine because we had several cats, one at least of whom never seemed to learn what house training was all about. Also there might be a piglet or two lying in a straw box near the Aga and trying out its funny wobbly legs on the slippery flagstone surface. These were the runts of the litters who, finding themselves left out in the cold, had begun to give up the struggle for existence. Sometimes the warmth of the kitchen revived them but sometimes they were too small and feeble to survive. On one occasion Evelyn and I sat up all night in an attempt to keep a whole litter alive by feeding them regularly with glucose, but by morning they were all stiff and cold and our night vigil had been in vain. However I tell the story partly to show how, at the beginning of the Pilsdon adventure, we all did anything there was to do. This is probably true of the start of all communities: it is only later that specialization creeps in.

Through the kitchen was the back-kitchen where much of the real hard work was done, and through there again was the janitor room and the laundry.

The janitor room housed three generations of janitors. The first one was a huge black affair with a large mouth and a voracious appetite. You just jammed anthracite down its throat and went on pouring. And there were mysterious rites known only to a few initiates whereby this black mass was poked down until a glowing red bar appeared at the bottom of the stove. If this delicate operation was not performed efficiently and regularly the janitor went out and there were no baths and no washing-up water until the acolyte of the janitor had stoked up again. One of these hot-water guardians was called Fred Henderson and he loved to tell, with unabashed grin, how he had once neglected his duties and been sternly reproved by Uncle with the words, "For forgetfulness there is no forgiveness." It was a strange and sad irony that, in later years, Uncle was himself to lose his memory.

In the janitor room, which was warm and dry, we had four large racks for hanging clothes and in wet weather they were always heavily laden, especially on Mondays and Wednesdays. Monday was for one of the house washes, mostly the men's clothes, and everything else that came into the laundry that day was plunged into soapy water: raincoats, overcoats, anoraks, overalls, everything that would go into water, and some things that would not, was immersed, scrubbed, and hung out to dry. Colour, lining, and stitchery were all sacrificed on the altar of hygiene. I once washed a three-piece grey pin-striped suit for a man who was going to a new job. He was devoted to his suit and had worn it right through the winter and it was with some difficulty that I extracted it from him. But when I was half-way through the procedure I was suddenly struck by the horrifying thought that, instead of merely being a shade cleaner after my efforts it might be three shades less wearable. However my luck held and Philip left us looking as spruce as though he were starting work at the Bank of England.

Wednesday was for sheets, pillow-cases, towels, coverlets, and, in the summer, blankets, and woe betide anyone who tried to do their personal washing on that day. One of the worst things that ever happened to me domestically at Pilsdon happened on a Wednesday. It had been a dry day but not hot and there was no breeze. I had hung all the linen out on the lines in the morning but by late afternoon none of it had dried so the lines were heavily laden with something like forty sheets and towels. I looked at the sky and decided it was going to be a fine night so I thought I would leave the washing where it was and it would be dry early the next day. However, that night a storm blew up and at five-thirty in the morning I woke to hear the wind howling round the house and the rain falling with a kind of sullen malice. I lay in bed for a little while shuddering with horror at the thought of the laundry lines until, able to bear it no longer, I slipped on a thick dressing-gown and wellingtons and sallied out to survey the damage. It was even worse than I had anticipated. Half the sheets were lying, thick with mud, on the sodden grass and half the rest were dancing about on the lines as though possessed, attached by only one peg and with frayed edges and torn hems flapping wildly. In a kind of stupor I gathered them all up and took them back to the laundry and then and there rewashed them all finishing just as the breakfast bell went at eight o'clock. Never again, I vowed, would I leave my washing out overnight. And I never have.

On one other occasion too I found that most of the clothes had been blown off the lines. This time it was a very cold frosty day but dry and sunny so they were still clean and unharmed, but one pair of pyjamas looked very comic. They had blown straight off against a small nearby tree and the arms of the jacket had wrapped themselves around it so that the trunk was firmly clasped in a pair of bloodless, striped, wincyette arms.

Most of us took a turn at doing the washing and when Anne worked in the laundry she was famous for her unintentional dyeing. The men's underwear came out pink one week and purple the next. They were magnificently uncomplaining. I sometimes wonder whether men know what they are wearing. They would come and ask you if you had seen a pair of brown socks and a grey shirt which you were supposed to have washed but, when finally unearthed, the socks might turn out to be green and the shirt blue with yellow stripes.

In the very early days of Pilsdon we had no washing machine and all the sheets were laid out on a big deal table, scrubbed by hand, and then boiled in the copper. Most of us who were relegated to this duty started straight after breakfast, hoping to be finished by lunch-time. Not so Maureen. She started at five o'clock in the evening, gathered her boy-friends around her, and the laundry became a kind of steamy night club with card games going on until the early hours of the morning. But the washing was done and it was cleaner than I usually managed to make it. In those days too the laundry was a sort of outhouse with a sloping corrugated roof which let in more rain than it kept out, but later years saw the laundry re-roofed and two washing machines installed. Grinding hard work was over, but so was some of the fun.

But perhaps one of the greatest uses of the laundry had nothing to do with washing at all. There was very little privacy at Pilsdon: the bedrooms all held either two or more people and the other rooms, the common room, the dining-room, the library, were all for public use. So the laundry often became the scene for the unburdening of troubles or the discussing of personal problems. Many a secret tear was shed there, partly perhaps because it was so steamy most of the time that red-rimmed eyes were less suspect there than anywhere else, and also the noise of the machines made conversation, if slightly difficult, at least relatively private. Whatever the reason, many a confidence was given and received in the laundry and many a tear was quietly wiped away.

## VII

The 'feel' of Pilsdon was further conditioned by its environment. We were essentially a rural, farming community, living in the heart of the country — six miles from the nearest town — and virtually self-supporting. We had cows, pigs, poultry, and a huge vegetable garden. Much of our life was spent outdoors both winter and summer. We also did all our own maintenance work and most of our own building and as Pilsdon always had a high percentage of men there was never any shortage of people with knowledge and experience of such things. Also, because ours was a country existence, our life and activities were strongly governed by the changing seasons. For many city dwellers the distinction between the seasons has almost ceased to exist. Men and women who spend all day in artificially cooled or heated offices have only a nodding acquaintance with summer and winter but in the country they have a strong individuality and influence both the day's work and the day's play.

Pilsdon was always beautiful but in spring it was breath-taking. Wild daffodils sprang up everywhere, Lewesdon hill was awash with bluebells and the strip of grass behind the house was lit by white narcissi. Pilsdon had long been famous for its wild daffodils. They grew in the fields and all the way along the bank of the stream between the house and the cottage. During our first years at Pilsdon people came in cars from far and near and ravaged the banks plundering ruthlessly and returning, their car boots laden with the fruits of their spoil. Sunday was raid day *par excellence* and after one or two Sundays the destruction was almost total. So we cogitated on how best to get rid of our undesirable predators. We contemplated putting up such notices as 'Beware. Lion on the loose' or 'Danger. Adders Plentiful' but decided that people were as likely to be taken in by these as by 'Haggis crossing' in Scotland. So finally we thought we would be polite and Anne made a beautifully hand-lettered notice board with the words 'please leave the flowers for others to enjoy' and, strangely perhaps, that did the trick and from then on our daffodils were allowed to grow and flourish undisturbed.

Spring was the gardener's marathon. There was so much planting to be done, hundreds of boxes of seedlings to be pricked out, the ground to be dug and turned and prepared for every conceivable kind of vegetable. We grew peas, and runner beans in tall arched cathedrals, brussel sprouts, cauliflowers, various kinds of cabbage including the red variety. We grew French beans as well as runners, and broad beans, onions, shallots, beetroot, parsnips, swedes, carrots, leeks, celery and celeriac, spinach, sweet corn, curly kale, purple and white sprouting broccoli, marrows, courgettes, lettuces, tomatoes, cucumbers, green peppers, herbs, and of course the inevitable potato. One year we experimented with pink fur apples, a variety of new potato which is to the average potato what a nectarine is to a peach, but the cleaning of them for a family of thirty made even the gourmets think twice before growing them again. Also one year we grew sugar peas but the same thing applied and the labour of shelling these miniscule green particles was not worth the delight of eating them.

In addition to all these vegetables we grew rhubarb, gooseberries, black and red currants, strawberries, raspberries, a few loganberries, melons in the small greenhouse, peaches occasionally on the peach tree, and even a late crop of strawberries and raspberries in the autumn. And in the front garden there were three wide herbaceous borders, rose beds, and a large cutting garden. And the spade work was all done, both literally and metaphorically, in the spring. The total labour force of Pilsdon was recruited and organized to deal with it.

And inside there was the usual spring-cleaning and at Pilsdon that often meant interior decoration. The white walls and ceilings were usually cream or even brown after the woodsmoke of the winter fires and a fresh coat of paint was urgently needed. Sometimes it was difficult with so many varying tastes to make a decision about colour. Percy always wanted white everywhere but some of us preferred warmer colours, or even wallpaper. A wayfarer whose trade had at one time been interior decorating was asked to paint the front hallway and stairs.

"You'se can keep all them other colours," he said belligerently, "ah wants pink and it's pink ah'm having."

Arguments, persuasion, commands, threats, all were equally unavailing — either the walls were going to be pink or he was off down the road and we could find someone else to do the work. So pink they eventually became and after a time we ceased to pay much attention to them just as we ceased to notice the rather strange collection of pinks and magnolia and beige which found its way into the dining-room.

For Christians spring means Easter, Easter is preceded in the church calendar by Lent, and Lent is introduced by Shrove Tuesday, known to most people as pancake day. I always seemed to be the cook on this occasion because it was Gillian's day off and so, whether it was my cooking week or not, Tuesday fell to my lot. It meant standing in front of the Aga for two hours pouring batter into the old iron frying pan and flicking the pancakes over. Tossing was out of the question even had I known how — the pan was too heavy. I was usually frantically decanting the last drops of batter when the first course was finishing. But I enjoyed it. It was a day when cooking was not just work but an age-old drama of feasting and a community is the perfect setting for such rituals.

Lent meant nothing to many of the people at Pilsdon but for those who cared there was a special service on Wednesday evenings with a sermon and usually Bible study and it was generally at this time of year that we had study weekends when a guest speaker would be invited to stay with us from Friday evening until Sunday and we had talks followed by group discussion, and much extra, unorganized, discussion in the kitchen and bedrooms afterwards.

And right through Lent the choir was busy lubricating its vocal chords for a full-length performance on Palm Sunday. The choir was not only an activity of the community but was also supported by people from outside. It was not a hand-picked group: hardly anyone who wanted to sing in it was refused although some people, after agonizing through one choir practice, chose to retire defeated. It was not always easy for ambitious baritones to realize that just singing the tune two octaves down was not exactly what was required. So we occasionally made some astonishing sounds. I was accustomed to choral idiosyncrasies. As a village choirmistress I had suffered from a bass who could only sing double bass and a tenor who was so fat that he had to take a breath after every three notes and so was always three notes behind. But when one man joined the Pilsdon choir and always sang soprano the sound had to be heard to be believed and I was quite unashamedly grateful that he only decided to stay with us a few weeks. But we also boasted some very good musicians — Hazel was a much better musician than I was myself but she was marvellously supportive of me and unfailingly loyal: never by word or look did she make me feel she knew much more about all things musical. Although she did. And Ruth, after leaving home, had her voice trained and was a very good soprano and our number one soloist. So the musical strength of the choir generally managed to outsing the more wayward elements. Friday nights was sacred to choir practice and the choristers were wonderfully regular in their attendance, the most gallant being Gladys Ewins who came to our very first practice and hardly missed more than half a dozen the whole of the next twenty years. She lived in a cottage in the Marshwood Vale and neither rain nor snow nor wind nor an arthritic hip could prevent her from walking a mile up the lane every Friday evening.

Good Friday was always a day of silence. Some people found this very strange and others found it embarrassing and one or two even disapproved of inflicting upon everyone, agnostics and atheists as well as Christians, something which belongs so specifically to the Christian heritage. It was only inside the house itself that Percy asked for silence to be kept: outside in the television rooms and in the pottery and gardens people were free to talk as they liked, but there were still a few who seemed to find it a virtual impossibility to remain silent, who perhaps lost their sense of identity with the loss of communication and felt like ciphers in a shadow land. But it was a day many of us looked forward to, a day of undisturbed peace and quietness when it was not considered rude and antisocial to hide away with our own thoughts and a book.

Spring, summer, autumn, and even winter, whenever the sun was bright and warm we ate our lunch outside, sitting on the grass or on the steps of the summer house or on the wide wooden garden seats which stood on the lawn in all weathers.

"Let's go and inspect the pitch," the cook would suggest with cheerful optimism to the person in charge of the dining-room. "I'll help you bring the things in again if it rains."

And out they would both go to feel the grass and cast a quizzical look at the sky.

But in summer the great outdoors became almost an addiction. Its two highlights were haymaking and beach parties. Our own hay was negligible but our neighbour had a dairy herd and about 180 acres of pasture land so he was grateful for our help and in return gave us some of the bales for our own use.

The haymaking was done in three shifts when the weather permitted, two people in the morning, two in the afternoon, and two more in the evening and, on the whole, setting aside the odd bit of grumbling which seems essential to life, it was one of the most popular of Pilsdon's activities. It still had a sort of old-fashioned glamour probably conjuring up fantasies of overflowing cider and rosy-cheeked dairymaids with rumpled petticoats, and there was also a sense of comradeship about it and much laughter and the satisfaction of a job well done. In the early years we often had foreign students staying with us and as this was generally during the summer holidays they always found themselves helping with the hay and you could hear their voices as they rode gaily on top of the bales from the fields to the barn. The huge Dutch barn was just behind our sheds and looked as though it belonged to us. Between it and our garage and workshop was a wide strip of grassy gravel where, one summer day, we had a cricket match. It was a four-a-side affair and I was deputed to be the umpire. They gave me six stones to transfer from one pocket to the other to count the balls in the overs but as there were rather a lot of no-balls and wides and I got excited the overs were of very uncertain duration. One masterly swing from one of the batsmen sent the ball spinning right over the rooftops into our grassy back quadrangle and only just missed the head of an innocent pigman going about his lawful duty, so in some quarters the cricket match was rather less than popular.

Beach parties too were comradely times. They were a regular feature of the fine summers and these seemed to be in the majority unless distance has lent enchantment to the view. They were arranged at lunch-time when we were all tucking into salad and home-made bread. Sometimes, if it was very hot, the house would be nearly emptied in the afternoon and three, or even four, carloads of men, women, and children went off in the direction of Charmouth, Eype, or Seatown. I was seldom a member of these expeditions preferring the peace of the house and garden when everyone else had gone but for most people the beach, like the hay, never failed in its appeal and one memorable year a group of enthusiasts went on taking a dip until well into November and again on a fine Christmas Day, but 'dip' was no misnomer and one girl in the party went in fully clothed, quite unable to face the idea of standing shiveringly half naked on a cold, wind-swept beach.

Summer was a time of lazy afternoons and busy evenings though mine were often busier perhaps than they should have been. Gill's metabolism seemed to get her off to a flying start first thing in the morning and that, coupled with the speed at which she worked, usually meant that she could put her feet up after supper. But I operate less well in the morning, or perhaps I am just much lazier, but whatever the reason I was usually pouring sticky jam into still stickier pots or boxing raspberries or slicing the interminable bean until nearly bedtime frantically helped by kind friends who saw the plight I was in.

That seemed to be the trouble with the summers: there was too much of everything — too many people in the dining-room, too much heat in the kitchen, too many beans to slice, too many blackcurrants to pick, too many parties to show round, too many cakes to bake, and too many clothes to wash. And above all there were too many wasps. They were the biggest plague of our summers. They invaded the kitchen in huge armies and descended on every bit of cake and biscuit in sight. And they positively lusted after chutney. We tried swatting them with newspapers: we tried trapping them in jars of diluted jam; and Uncle went round after dark with a spoon tied to a very long stick poisoning them at source. But they kept coming. I hope there are no wasps in heaven. It quite spoils the idea of paradisal summerland.

To add to the other hazards of summer we often ran short of water, although this was liable to occur at any time of the year. We had our own reservoir in the hills behind the house which was fed by a spring which everyone in the neighbourhood assured us had never run dry. It is probably true that there was nothing wrong with the spring but sometimes we failed to communicate with it. The first ominous sign would be the cold water running chocolate brown out of the tap and then there would be a decreased pressure in the flow, after which somebody was sent out with a pair of binoculars to read the gauge. We had this rigged up on the reservoir and with the help of strong field-glasses it could be seen from the house if you knew where to look for it. If the marker was low — and the portents rarely played false —

someone had to go up to the reservoir to investigate the situation. Probably there was a leak somewhere in one of the long pipes running down to the house and there would be an ominous puddle in one of the fields betraying the whereabouts of the crack or break. But sometimes it was merely that our neighbour's cows had been thirstier than usual, and we supplied several of our neighbours with water. Or sometimes, woe betide the culprit, a tap had been left on all night at one of the troughs. But, whatever the cause, the outcome was plain enough — the reservoir was empty and we had no water. So a ban was immediately put on baths, clothes washing, hair washing, washing-up, and the pulling of lavatory chains. Two men went scurrying round to a neighbour with empty churns which came back full of clean drinking water, and two or three more opened up the well which we had found in the courtyard and with a bucket and string hauled up water for other purposes. If the weather was hot swimming helped with the general hygiene but there were great sighs of relief when the word went round 'O.K. for baths again'.

Sometimes this drought continued for two or three days depending on the reason for it and how soon we located the leak, but once this was mended all that was necessary was patience and, with our water turned off, the reservoir filled up again quite quickly. But one of the Pilsdon jobs was always cleaning the reservoir and the filter beds. Two people were generally deputed to do this together and in warm weather it was a pleasant enough occupation.

The summer was undoubtedly our busiest time partly because it brought so many extra visitors and the house was always overflowing. But I think our guests liked the summer best. There was always plenty to do and plenty of people to do it with; the garden was beautiful, the sun often hot, and life was lived mostly out of doors; the countryside was green, the lanes dry underfoot, and the frequent outings to the sea were a diversion and a welcome change of scenery.

In the summer the vegetable garden and greenhouse also flourished and if we sometimes complained that the bean rows were too close or that there were too many of them or that the damp weather had ruined the strawberries, we had to complain about something and it did not affect the pleasure of eating corn-on-the-cob straight from its long green lines or lettuces that, ten minutes before, had been in the soil. Lunch in the summer nearly always consisted of our own vegetables, lettuce salad with grated cheese and hard boiled egg, or marrow either with tomatoes or in cheese sauce, runner beans with hard-boiled egg, the small carrot thinnings with baby turnips, spinach and cheese, or just peas delicious on their own with parsley butter. There was an infinite variety and we never tired of it. And always on the table as an extra would be a large bowl of tiny, sweet Gardener's Delight tomatoes which were so plentiful that we ate them at every meal.

In the strawberry season we were utterly spoilt. There were usually so many that we had them every other night for supper alternating with fresh raspberries, a huge bowlful topped with a spoonful of our own whipped cream. For most of us this was a gourmet's paradise but some of the men, who were partial to steam puddings and stodge at any time of the year, could be heard towards the end of the strawberry season muttering under their breath "not just strawberries again!" But I hasten to add here that there was virtually no grumbling about food. If the steam pudding had collapsed in the middle everybody said they liked their pudding mushy, and if the bread was burnt they said charcoal was good for you. They were kind and loyal and a joy to cook for.

The flower garden was always beautiful but in the summer it was a riot of colour. It was an old walled garden with wide herbaceous borders down two sides of a large lawn in one corner of which was a small pond half circled by a rockery. Nearer the house were rose beds and a luxuriant straggling Albertine which trailed its pink arms over one of the walls and over an archway leading to the road. Underneath the windows of the house and against its walls grew more roses, wisteria, a magnolia tree, and a red japonica which was always full of the hum of bees. In the evening when the old stone wall was touched with dying pink all the colours seemed to radiate a light of their own: the power of the midday sun diminished their glory but twilight enhanced and enriched it. There was a summer house which had once revolved on the lawn just outside the windows and here people would sit, alone or in groups, whenever they had time to relax, and often it would be occupied until late on a summer evening: people could hardly bear to drag themselves away from the peace and the scented warmth. Perhaps some people may remember Pilsdon best for its beauty — the gentle fields spreading away from the house on all sides, the narrow quiet lanes, the complete absence of bus or train or factory chimney, and everywhere flowers, flowers of the hedgerow, primroses, daffodils, bluebells, meadow sweet, campion, wood anemones, a large garden full of flowers, and always flowers beautifully arranged in every room of the house.

And yet sometimes this beauty and this peace would be in striking contrast to the tortured unrest and mental turmoil of some of the people we had staying with us. The warmth of the sun did not relax them and the beauty found no reflection in eyes which were blinded by the dark shadows of their own fears and guilts. It was always sad to see a woman sitting in a deck-chair on the lawn twisting her handkerchief compulsively, her body set into lines of rigid tension even while it assumed an attitude of ease; or a man with hollow eyes pacing up and down the garden paths chased by his own furies and unable to receive any impressions from the outside world. And it was sometimes difficult for us to give up our own selfish enjoyment of the sun or an hour's hard-won privacy, or even to get outside our own problems sufficiently to give full attention to the anguished and despairing especially when the giving only increased the desire for more. So sometimes the springs of compassion turned to irritation and frustration at the strength of the unlit places of the mind and our own inability to help or heal.

The summer moved on to autumn and autumn at Pilsdon meant the Anniversary. Everything else was secondary to preparations for it. We had bought the house on October 16th 1958 and we considered that date to be the Pilsdon birthday and every year we invited our friends and neighbours from a radius of about thirty miles to our birthday party. This took place mostly in the evening and consisted of a service with a visiting preacher followed by a buffet supper in the house and then an informal concert in what we rather grandiosely called our 'theatre', a home-made concert in which the choir figured prominently. Then there were solos by Ruth and, when they were with us, Rosemary, Nick and Michael, trios, quartets, and octets, usually vocal, guitar solos by Trevor and Doug, side-splitting stories in broad Dorset by our solicitor and friend, Mr Scott-Rowe, Scott Joplin on the piano by Trevor, Victorian piano duets by Hazel and me dressed up in Laura Ashley Victoriana, splendid renderings of Flanders and Swann by Miles and Trevor and, once, Rossini's cat duet by Ruth and Mike complete with masks and whiskers. They were happy concerts full of fun and laughter, and if the sopranos were sometimes a little flat or the basses a little sharp what did that matter when everybody was having such a good time. So, throughout September and most of October we were planning our party, and in November we were recovering from it.

The food for the party generally consisted of chicken pie or chicken curry followed by a most delicious blackberry mousse of Gillian's concocting. It was this mousse which dictated our autumn activities because it required about sixteen pints of undiluted blackberry juice, so blackberry picking was the order of the day in September and parties of pickers, both conscientious and not so conscientious, set off in the afternoons along every lane, and although there is a country saying that the devil is in the blackberries in October we paid scant heed to the possible machinations of that redoubtable personage and October found us still picking and still scouring every bush and hedgerow for those last luscious berries. When picked they were all thrown into large saucepans, heated, squashed down, and then hung in large muslin bags in the larder to strain out the last drop of juice. For many years this was caught in great china basins, white ones with designs of flowers and dragons round the outside. We had chamber pots to match them but I am not quite sure what happened to those. The bowls were the kind that used to stand with their ewers on plain deal well-scrubbed washstands in attic bedrooms but now can only be found elegantly reclining in the showrooms of smart antique shops and you have to pay a fortune for them. I think their original owners would turn in their graves if they could see the price tags on them now.

The musicians too were busy throughout September preparing music both for the service and the concert. The anthem in the church was sometimes part of a cantata or extended anthem like the Handel Chandos Anthems and our most successful effort was 'The Song of Thanksgiving' by Vaughan Williams. But one of our most memorable attempts was Haydn's Te Deum. This is a splendid piece lasting about ten minutes, with great variety of mood, and all went very well until we came to the fugal ending. We persevered manfully as the threads of sound began to unravel and I waved my arms with grim cheerfulness as each part took the bit between its teeth and raced around the musical course. However we all met up a page or two before the end and raised the roof with a triumphant final C. Afterwards, at the concert, we swung into 'Jonah-man Jazz' one year, 'Joseph and his amazing technicolour dream-coat' another year, 'The Daniel Jazz', and 'Captain Noah and his Floating Zoo' complete with a hilarious moving scenario of animals, a huge ark with a magnificent giraffe looking out through the window, and an illuminated rainbow. And one memorable year we tried to make a film to illustrate some honky-tonk songs we were singing. Armed with the necessary equipment the camera crew and would-be stars set off for Charmouth where we astonished the residents by parading up and down the beach in Edwardian gear to the taped sounds of 'Oh, I do like to be beside the sea-side' and 'There's something about a soldier'. We even went as far afield as Castle Cary in Somerset where we had heard of brothers who owned a tandem. We begged the loan of it, took it out into a country lane and spent hours teaching Pam and Ted how to ride it and then waiting for the sun to come out so that they could sail away down the lane to the strains of 'Daisy, Daisy'. We were very pleased with ourselves and shouted out things like "Cut" and "Pan round", thoroughly enjoying the fantasy of being film-makers, but unfortunately, by the time it was all finished and had been sent for processing it was not back for the concert, so we showed it in private in the library afterwards and found it was much funnier played backwards with the tandem floating weightlessly uphill.

Autumn too was the season of the apple harvest and at one time Pilsdon had a fair sized orchard from which the apples were picked and stowed away in the apple loft, the room which later became an extension of the pottery. Whether the pottery 'ghost' had once lived on apples I do not know but if he did perhaps his later prowlings were due to a not unnatural resentment at the change.

Some of our trees bore cider apples and in the old barn behind the house was a large disused cider press which moulded and rotted away there for twenty years. We never used the cider apples ourselves but one day Gillian was horrified to find a cow in the last stages of what looked like some dread bovine desease. A frantic telephone call to the vet brought him skidding to our door.

"She's drunk," he said with a wry smile, "just take her out of the orchard."

James Herriot himself could not have supplied our alcoholics with more to laugh about.

In this orchard too we once berthed a gipsy caravan. It was a picturesque sight as you came up the drive to the house and its owner was no less picturesque with splendid dark eyes and long black hair. But it was advisable not to go too near without a little caution. The horse grazed peacefully near the front door of this home on wheels, but a big black dog who lived round the back would have taken a chunk out of your calf without a second's warning — and did, on one occasion.

Later, we cut all these fruit trees down: their fruit-bearing days were over. And here the Pilsdon herd grazed peacefully and soberly and sometimes, in the summer, the field sported a tent or two, housing overflow guests from an already overcrowded house.

It was usually after the Anniversary that we started having fires in the house.

"Just a small one, Les," Percy would say, and Les, muttering a little under his breath about sun and wind and rain and snow and such allied and controversial matters, would start to pile the logs in the big log basket that lived outside the common room door and chop sticks for kindling in preparation for his annual winter creations — the fire.

1963. The year of the Great Snow. It was the most memorable of all the Pilsdon winters. I can remember every face from that extraordinary time. Prisoners on a small island bounded by deep snow, we grew close. Inactivity and boredom could so easily have rocked the boat; tempers could have been short and the atmosphere one of tension and hostility. But it was the reverse that happened and the friendships made that winter have never been forgotten.

The cook was in a luxury position. The Aga kept the kitchen permanently warm and relatively cosy, but all the other rooms were freezing especially the bedrooms. In those days we had no central heating and our attic bedroom was so icy that we hardly ever visited it except to take a flying leap into bed. Unbelievably I turned the hot-water bottles out of bed on to the floor one morning, and going back there after breakfast, found the water inside them frozen solid. We were right under the roof and the woodwork was very old and much of it had rotted badly. The draughts were so plentiful and so extensive that we sometimes felt as though we were living outside. One particularly bad area was what we called the glory hole. This was an extension of our room into the roof space, separated from us by only a badly fitting door. It was a useful storage space but filled with cracks and crevices through which the wind whistled mercilessly.

Our attic room was perhaps an extreme case but all the rooms were cold in this seventeenth-century house, and all the corridors were draughty, the only exceptions being the kitchen and the common room. Here, in this large beautifully panelled room, we all gathered to while away the time, give each other the latest reports from the cold front, and warm our frozen feet and hands when snow shovelling was temporarily suspended.

For most people this was the only available activity. The more energetic shovelled from early morning until it was too dark to see even the snow, with occasional breaks for carrying ice for thawing from what had once been a stream. The lazier ones shovelled for an hour or so in the morning and then retired to the common room for a smoke which managed to last them most of the rest of the day.

The pipes, both the house pipes and also those running down the hillside from our reservoir, were a daily disaster and the busiest person at Pilsdon was Tom who worked ceaselessly night and day ensuring that our water supply was kept running more or less constantly and that the flooding was of minor rather than major proportions. Without Tom I doubt whether we should have survived the winter at all. He was a precision tool-maker and on one of his visits to Pilsdon he made us all beautiful bracelets out of some old copper which he found in a shed at the back of the house. He also had a flair for black and white line drawings and I still have a picture of an old tithe barn in Somerset which I badgered him into giving me. Unfortunately he also had a taste for alcohol, or at least for the effects of it, and this fairly effectively prevented him from the full exercise of any of his talents. But for a few months in the winter of 1963 he had time and attention for nothing but plumbing.

For the first ten days of the snow we were completely isolated and even without the use of the telephone. We ran short of bread as did our neighbours, so a walk was organized across the fields to the village of Marshwood. Six people decided to go and with sacks over their shoulders, gloves, mufflers, several pullovers, wellington boots and a few stout sticks they set off immediately after breakfast. I was the cook that week and the thick soup which was to be our lunch was almost ready to be served when the party returned. They fell on to the kitchen chairs in a state of complete exhaustion. The snow had been three feet deep most of the way, sometimes more, and it had been a struggle lifting each foot. The actual distance they had covered could not have been more than three miles but it had taken them four hours to do it. The comedy of the situation came when the bread was emptied out of the sacks on to the kitchen floor. The loaves were black. They had taken coal sacks and every loaf had to be washed before being put into the oven to crisp them up again.

For weeks we hardly left the house and grounds and nobody visited us, although one day a cowboy whom we called Haggis was blown in out of the snow. He had been walking round and round trying desperately to find the house and his feet were all but frost-bitten. They were very painful and it was a long time before he was able to walk properly. And a Chinese friend of ours who had come on a short visit was trapped with us and had to stay much longer than she had intended. She must have suffered intensely from the cold, and when we did finally manage to get her out through the snow she caught a chill which subsequently turned into pneumonia and had to spend some time in a London hospital.

On Sunday nobody came to Evensong in the little chapel which was only just outside our garden wall, so we held the service in the common room in front of a roaring log fire, and nearly the whole house attended. Whether this was due to the informality of the setting or the warmth of the room — churches are notoriously cold places — or to the increased friendliness existing between us, I do not know, but the deep-chested singing of the men was something not often heard in any church.

The deepest voice of all belonged to one of Pilsdon's best loved characters. Fred had been born and brought up at Lerwick in the Shetland Isles and had lived for many years on the sea before falling a victim to the enticements of alcohol and so joining the wayfaring tribe known to us as cowboys. We called him the King of the Cowboys, a title he earned partly because of his own intelligence and independence of spirit, and partly because he seemed to know every member of the tribe and to be their own unacknowledged leader.

As a raconteur Fred had few equals and throughout that long winter he delighted us every evening with tales of his boyhood in the Shetlands and of his experiences on the road. Several of his stories featured an aunt who had lived near them when he was a child. This delightful lady had possessed only two teeth, one top right and the other bottom left, and Fred mimicked her extraordinary grimaces as she tried to lock them together in a pickled onion. She was a lady of considerable girth and when she decided it was time for her to get married, she lifted a tiny man called Andy by the breeches from the neighbouring garden and put him down on her side of the fence saying, "We're spliced."

True or not, these tales were graphically told and we lapped them up as we sat toasting our toes and faces and trying to ignore the small draughts which trickled down our backs and along our shoulder blades.

Meanwhile food for the livestock was running short and we were worried about them. There were terrible stories from Exmoor and Dartmoor of sheep and ponies dying from starvation and exposure and we wondered what we were going to do to feed our own animals. Telephone calls were made but it seemed impossible to get supplies through to us. Finally we heard that a helicopter had been detailed to drop the food to us and we awaited its arrival in excited anticipation. However, just before it was due to reach us a three-ton lorry managed to come part way towards us and we were able to meet it and transfer the load into our own van. The day had been saved but we were a little disappointed not to have had the excitement of a helicopter landing.

Nobody was ashamed that winter to ask for long johns from the Pilsdon cupboard and very soon our supplies of woollen long johns and vests were completely exhausted. One man became the proud possessor of a splendid pair of ribbed, hand-knitted grey ones. The long johns had stretched so much in repeated washings that they came right up to his arm-pits. Most people wore their pyjamas as well under their trousers and even inside the house many men were still in overcoats and mufflers. Gill and I managed to acquire some very thick wool and with this we embarked on a crash knitting campaign: knitted mittens and woolly hats followed each other in non-stop sequence, and other people's needles were clicking fast.

We also acquired two pairs of skis and some of us made our first tentative essays in skiing on the sloping fields behind the house. Most of them had a fairly gentle gradient and were an ideal nursery playground for beginners. But one Sunday afternoon Percy badly sprained a tendon and had to be half carried by Ruth from the hill, and after this the interest in skiing waned a little and we reverted to walking out each day to review the state of the snow and to feast our eyes on its astonishing beauty, and the strange sight of our lane buried beneath twenty feet of it. The hedges had disappeared and the snow had climbed up on one side almost to the height of the telegraph poles. And this was West Dorset, only four miles as the crow flies from the warming surge of the English Channel. But the narrowness of the lanes and the height of the hedges as well as the driving force of the winds had trapped the snow as securely as the snow had trapped us.

Slowly the winter passed: the snowfalls became less frequent and a thaw began to set in. Snow ploughs eventually found their way to us, but we later heard from the roads department that we were the last place in England to be freed. It was then April.

The winter was over and so was our close-knit friendship. People began to drift away, to find work, or back to their homes and families, and new faces came with the coming of spring. But the winter was not easily forgotten and neither was the band of men and women who had shared its rigours and its challenge.

## VIII

Festivals are as old as time and occur in every known culture and civilization. They are age-old dramas of feasting and music and the giving of gifts. They represent the social aspect of our lives and activities and our need for excitement, colour, and variety. And they seem especially significant in the country where life is not studded with bright lights or the dazzle of the latest trendiness.

At Pilsdon we celebrated them to the full.

Christmas was not just a festival but almost another season. It started in November when knitting became an obsession with the women. The men laughed but the earnest needle-clicking never stopped. It was an accompaniment to everything — except the guillotine. Scarves, gloves, pullovers, socks, Balaclava helmets, and mittens accumulated and were hidden away in drawers and suitcases, under beds, and on the tops of tall wardrobes. Shopping expeditions too assumed gigantic proportions and we started going further afield to such towns as Taunton and Exeter in search of the big stores with their more comprehensive array of goods. And decorating the house was not just an affair of putting up a few streamers and hanging a bit of holly and mistletoe here and there but a sophisticated art which took weeks to prepare. Last year's box of carefully preserved tinselled goodies was brought down from the attics and the artists and conscripted would-be artists gathered around in the library like vultures to take their pick of straw angels and stars, skeletal wreaths, coloured paper, polystyrene backing sheets, plastic berries, and Christmas roses. And the result transformed the whole house into a kind of magic grotto. There was always a large and very beautiful crib in the library, and there were stained glass windows made of tissue paper, exotic wreaths sprayed with silver and gold paint, mobiles of straw angels and straw stars, and highly artistic friezes of every kind including, one year, cut-outs in black silhouette of the twelve days of Christmas complete with the most animated pipers piping and lords a-leaping.

In Christmas week itself there was our own service of nine lessons and carols when the tiny church was at its most beautiful, packed to the doors and glowing in the light of over a hundred candles. This was followed by a party in the common room with ham sandwiches and mince pies and coffee for all, and more, community carols, round the fire. And we also gave a party for our own children and those of the entire neighbourhood. Both these parties made a lot of extra work in the kitchen. A dozen loaves were made into sandwiches, packed up in foil, and stored away in the freezer, and three or four hundred mince pies were put into tins and polythene containers and hidden in the store room for reheating on the night of the party. And for the children there were home-made cakes and meringues and sausage rolls and biscuits, and every year we racked our brains trying to decide on an entertainment, a conjuror, or Punch and Judy, or films, or a home-brewed pantomime. One year we decided on the last and it turned into the story of St Nicholas with a realistic portrayal of three small children drowning in a butt of malmsey but, as in all good stories, they were rescued at the eleventh hour by the saint himself and went dancing round the stage in high glee.

The choir was nearly always invited to give a carol concert before or just after Christmas in one of the nearby towns or villages. One never-to-be-forgotten occasion we had all trooped in and taken our places. The chief tenor was missing and the other tenors relied on him heavily. He was a farmer and had phoned to say that he had a cow calving and was likely to be a little late. I waited as long as I dared but the audience was growing restive and I knew we must start singing. Desperately I played for time. I lengthened my opening speech and then, with sudden inspiration, announced that we would sing two community carols. At the end of all four verses of 'O little town of Bethlehem' our tenor was still not with us so we started on 'Once in royal David's city' — six verses if you do it all. At the end of the fourth verse he had still not arrived and I was breaking out in a cold sweat but in the last line of verse five there was a click of the door and a familiar smiling figure strode in. I have never sung the sixth verse with such abandon.

The midnight service was, for many people, the highlight of Christmas, this quiet communion at which over a hundred men and women moved up the aisle of the tiny church in silent procession and knelt at the communion rail with outstretched hands. My memory is of a great silence. There must have been some coughing and fidgeting and the rustle of pages being turned and the sound of footsteps on the stone floor, quiet words were being spoken at the altar and my hands were moving softly over the piano keys, but all this seemed to intensify the stillness. The only other occasion which affected me in the same way was the communion service we had on Maundy Thursday in the evening and on that day too the church was awe-inspiringly beautiful. Dressed all in white it looked bridal with white flowers and a filmy white veil covering the cross and tall white candles on either side of the altar. This service too had for me a quality of unearthly stillness which is the nearest thing I know to pure worship.

Whatever the demythologists may say about Christmas, whether there is any truth in the legend of Christ's birth or not, and whatever cynics may say about the commercialization of the festival seems to me to matter little: there is a need in the human soul for festivals and Christmas is one of the most magical. Every Christmas I catch my breath when I hear sung that anonymous medieval poem which is so beautiful that it seems like a miracle.

I sing of a maiden
That is makeless;
King of all kings
To her son she ches.

He came all so still
Where his mother was,
As dew in April
That falleth on the grass.

He came all so still
To his mother's bow'r,
As dew in April
That falleth on the flower.

He came all so still
Where his mother lay,
As dew in April
That falleth on the spray.

Mother and maiden
Was never none but she;
Well may such a lady
Godes mother be.

Beauty such as this is its own truth.

Christmas Day itself was riotous, especially in the morning when everybody was giving presents to everybody else and the whole house echoed to shouts of:

"Where's Bill? Anyone seen him?"

"Whatever's happened to Frank? He was here just a minute ago."

"I'm sure I had your present here but I seem to have lost it. Just hold on a moment and I'll pop upstairs."

"Hey, don't disappear" — frantic searching in a Father Christmas-sized bag — "Here it is, and could you give this to Sarah when you see her?"

And we were hilarious again at tea-time when everyone was given presents from the huge Christmas tree and joke presents were the order of the day. One rather cold winter a man had expressed a desire for a pair of tartan long johns. So Anne's boutique was rummaged for the required garment and a plain white woolly pair was unearthed. Whereupon Evelyn proceeded with coloured wool to tartanize them and when the man opened his present from the tree out fell a pair of beautiful plaid long johns which, amidst roars of merriment, he donned and wore for the rest of the evening.

We had extra guests with us over Christmas — our own family was always with us, Ruth and Mike, and our grandchildren, Becky and Justin — and friends who came in just for Christmas tea and Christmas dinner to share in a family meal and the family fun. But the truth is that it was not fun for everybody. One year we had with us a little old woman who had come in off the roads. She was very shy and quiet and withdrawn and mostly sat upstairs by herself on her bed. We gave her presents, things like woollen gloves and a muffler which we thought she might find useful when she left us again but the next day she quietly and gently gave them all back to us and went on her way as simply and anonymously as she had come.

And one year a woman who was a bad alcoholic came to us just before Christmas and we spent a large part of Christmas evening trying to persuade her not to go out and find the nearest pub. We succeeded for that night but not long afterwards she left us and, in the early spring, she was found dead of exposure on the Embankment in London. As a friend whose son died in the spring said to me:

"It seems almost worse to die when everything else is coming to life."

So it was not everyone who enjoyed Christmas. There were some who, deprived of their own families, almost hated it and others who, indifferent to its religious significance, disliked the excessive emotionalism and the general disturbance it created. I think those of us who participated most in its preparations were not always sufficiently sensitive to the feelings it aroused in the sad or the lonely or the cynical: we were too carried away by what Percy sometimes referred to as Christmas mania. There is always an area of selfishness in giving, and kindness can be suffocating, however well meant. So, for some, it was almost with a sigh of relief that Christmas slipped away and life once more returned to normal.

# Part Two

## The People

## IX

Some people will always remember Pilsdon for the fun that was so often rippling over the surface but although there was much laughter in our life together there was also deep sadness. Most, though by no means all, of our 'guests' were weighed down by an almost insupportable burden. Men and women, boys and girls – they came to us with problems of every kind, some labelled by psychiatrists as psychotic, some tarred with the brush of social disgrace, some haunted by guilt real or imaginary, and all of them unsure both of themselves and of their place in life. And these variegated troubles were not always alleviated by the offer of friendship, the satisfaction of communal work or the healthy open-air existence. This is by no means a 100% success story. The problems weighed people down too heavily for instant cure or speedy relief.

There is a girl sitting in the Pilsdon garden. She is writing a letter. Come and look over her shoulder. She will not mind. She is any girl of the many, many girls who have stayed at Pilsdon. She writes:

I had always thought of myself as a failure. Psychotherapists say that most people do but for me it was a very personal and private thing. I found it difficult to explain to anyone else. I even found it difficult to explain to myself. I was a fully qualified, trained nurse and enjoyed my work, but even though I was busy much of the time there was a large gap somewhere inside me which nothing seemed to fill. I did have a few friends but they all seemed so much more vivacious and self-confident than me and I felt a bit of a plain Jane in their company. I had even had one or two boy-friends but I was always a bit afraid of them and they found girls who were less inhibited and lost interest in me.

I tried hard to reason myself out of these feelings. I told myself they were childish and silly and there was no good reason for them. I was as intelligent as most of the girls I knew; I had a good steady job which I enjoyed, and I was not bad looking. I had a reasonably good figure, took a size 10 or 12 in clothes, and my face, although not up to Hollywood standards, was what people called pleasant.

Why then did I have this constant sense of failure and inadequacy which dogged me and prevented me from enjoying anything to the full, and made me envious of nearly every other girl I met? There was no answer, and my thoughts swam round and round in a stagnant pool until I felt like smashing my fist through the nearest window.

Well, the feelings escalated and things went from bad to worse until I was hardly able to concentrate even when I was at work on the wards. I became obsessed by this sense of failure and felt it was written on my face for all the world to see. I had become very withdrawn and found it difficult to accept friendship even when it was offered to me, so that I finally found myself sitting in a psychiatrist's office accepting his advice to go as a voluntary patient to the clinic of our nearest mental hospital.

There I was given electric shock treatment and I joined other patients in group therapy sessions and slowly, very slowly, I began to feel less trapped within myself. Obviously my feelings were not as personal or as private as I had thought: other people were paralysed by them too, and some had even worse problems, such ghastly troubles that I wondered how they had survived at all.

After about six months I had recovered sufficiently to be able to take an interest in life again. I talked to some of the other patients and wrote letters to my friends. I was still not quite ready to face the world again and to go back to my job but I wanted to live a more normal life than was possible in the hospital, and to begin to try out my new and fledgling feelings of greater self-confidence and my newly acquired knowledge that I was not alone in my troubles. Where else could I go? What should I do next?

It was at this point that a social welfare worker told me about Pilsdon. Here was the bridge I needed, she said, between life in the hospital and life in the world outside. It was a big house in the country, she explained, where people just like me could go if there was room, and people with other problems too, where everybody lived and worked together on a big farm and where nobody was considered odd or looked down on because they had spent some time in a mental hospital or found it difficult to cope with their problems. She would show me a booklet she had about the community and I could read it and then decide for myself whether I thought I would like to go there if they could have me.

And so it was that I found myself one June day in the compartment of an Inter-City train bound for Axminster in Devon. There I was greeted by a young man with a friendly smile and relieved of my luggage, and a few minutes after my train had pulled in we were off on the open country road with a view on my right across fields towards the sea.

I was a bit nervous and edgy but the young man chatted cheerfully and soon

we were descending a steep hill where the road was so narrow that the summer hedgerows almost met in the middle. Then, at the bottom of the hill, the country opened out a little and I saw a large grey house with a huge crop of outbuildings and a field in which some brown and white cows were grazing.
I was at Pilsdon . . . .

Arrival at Pilsdon might do nothing at first to dispel a person's gloom or anxiety and make them feel less threatened. They might even feel more so. If you arrived in the middle of the afternoon, a likely enough time, even though someone would have been detailed to show you round and try to make you feel welcome, you would still feel lost and strange. You might not be used to the country and feel conscious of having city clothes, a city voice, and city tastes. How could you possibly stand the silence of the fields all around, the complete absence apparently of shops and the exposure of being in such close proximity to thirty people instead of being anonymous in a huge crowd? And what about the work that might be expected of you? You had never done any gardening, never even seen a large vegetable garden, and cows frightened you.

After swallowing this terrifying pill there would be tea and supper when you had to run the gauntlet of thirty pairs of curious eyes all trained on you — or that is how it would feel — and the boisterous conversation would probably not be trimmed at all to your shyness and ignorance of the communal news-reel. The food too might be different from anything you were accustomed to — spinach and celeriac and kale and purple sprouting broccoli — not at all the kind of thing you bought at home or even thought of buying. And after supper was over there would still be a long lonely stretch of evening before you could cry your first tears into a strange pillow.

It always took several days to get used to living at Pilsdon. Sometimes it took very much longer and sometimes people never managed to adapt themselves to such a different environment. People's problems were real and deep and often chronic. Whatever the cause of psychic depression for instance, whether it is physical or mental or both, and whether it relates to something in a person's past experience or whether it is connected with birth trauma or pre-birth trauma or even with the events (as some people would think) of a previous earth existence, it is a terrible affliction and to tell anyone to snap out of it or to pull themselves together is as useless as catching air in a butterfly net. The conventional religious platitudes like 'count your blessings' or 'try to think of others rather than yourself' are equally useless or, at best, only temporary alleviations. The person concerned very often wants desperately to do just those things but it all seems so hopeless and the motivation for trying non-existent. Hope is perhaps the relevant word — not facile optimism, which sometimes looks like it, but the deep-seated conviction that life means something and that the meaning is good. This seemed to be a foreign country to so many people.

I am aware that the vast majority of men and women have no conscious awareness of this kind of hope nor do they become depressives just as most people who drink do not become alcoholics. But this gets nobody anywhere. I also know there is a theory that this illness, like many other seemingly mental ones, is caused by some chemistry of the body and is physical in origin and can be cured by a change of diet, and there is always the so-called Freudian theory that a happy and fulfilled sex life will cure everything. But I believe the roots of our lives are deeper and more complex than this and there are no easy answers to any of our problems. Certainly we never found any at Pilsdon. Perhaps this was one of the big things we learnt, that there is no simple answer to anything. This was borne in on us more and more forcibly as our experience grew. So many people lived in such darkness: they needed light but the switch seemed hidden. Some did find it and light slowly filled the dark places of their minds. But for some the darkness deepened and a few who had been with us at Pilsdon later opted for what they hoped would be the oblivion of a fatal overdose.

Many of those who came to us for help had withdrawn from any perceptible contact with reality or with the world. In the former case they had often been labelled schizophrenic: in the latter instance they had usually received no label but they had nearly all spent weeks, months, or even years in mental hospitals. They all seemed to have suffered from some too-harsh contact with reality, a sudden emotional shock or perhaps a sustained lack of emotional warmth and they had shut themselves in with their own bitterness and anger or with their own fantasies until they found themselves almost incapable of communication. They had retreated behind closed doors and the silence was almost total. Several times we had men and women staying with us who hardly spoke a word for months on end. They were like wounded animals curled up in silent misery. It was difficult but we tried not to pressurize them and slowly, very slowly, the almost concussive state passed and they returned, first to us, and then to the outside world.

Men and women who came to us from hospitals usually came loaded with drugs of every kind. One of Gill's favourite stories was of a lady who kept forgetting where she had put her amnesia tablets. When these people arrived they were supposed to off-load their pills onto us and they were then kept usually by Percy or Gill who gave them out in daily or possibly three day doses, one of the difficulties with so many pills being that, inevitably not all of them were handed in so that we sometimes had people taking overdoses, though not fatal ones, either of their own tablets or ones they had taken from someone else's drawers or handbag. Amazingly, considering how many people were taking pills, this happened relatively infrequently but often enough to keep us constantly aware of the danger.

Another, and perhaps greater, drawback to this cartload of drugs was that they dulled the sensibilities of their takers and so took the edge off much of what we were trying to do at Pilsdon. It is not true that we were letting people act out their fears and fantasies: the full effect of this kind of therapy might have had a detrimental effect on a small close-knit community such as ours, and also we were not trained for this sort of thing. But we did offer people space to try to come to grips with their problems, space for a greater degree of self-awareness and an alleviation of some of the inhibiting pressures of life, and an area of freedom to be at least a little eccentric in dress and behaviour so long as the basic social pattern was not destructive. But a sleep-walking schizophrenic or a comatose depressive was unable to participate in this spatial dimension, and yet we did also realize that without the drugs we might have been unable to have them at Pilsdon at all.

The alcoholics and other addictives who came to us were better able to benefit once the effects of their addiction had at least partially worn off, but they tended consciously to lay aside their problem while they were with us only to find it waiting for them again once they had left and were facing the same situation which they had unsuccessfully tried to cope with before. While they were at Pilsdon it was relatively easy for some of them to do this: there was no alcohol on the premises and the nearest pub was two miles away down what was often a wet and muddy lane, and as the rule about drinking was strict they knew they would not be welcome back if they transgressed it. So, many alcoholics at Pilsdon enjoyed a respite from their troubles and some even tried to pretend to themselves and others that they did not exist. "Drinking has never been my problem," said one man as he raised his tea cup with a shaking hand. Just occasionally, and especially at the beginning, we did have trouble with men returning from a session at Shave Cross pub. Sometimes they would be sentimental and amorous but more often they were angry and ready to pick a fight with the first person who crossed their path and as this was often Percy waiting for them to come back he had to rule with a pretty firm hand. But the instances lessened as time went on and the traditions of Pilsdon became established and people saw the advantages of being a 'dry' house. None of us were teetotallers by principle but our abstention certainly helped the alcoholics who lived in our midst.

One of the most distressing nervous illnesses is agoraphobia. It seems to afflict women more than men perhaps because its roots appear to be emotional. It is especially distressing because it so curtails and restricts the activities of an otherwise normal person. We had agoraphobics at Pilsdon who were afraid to go through the front door alone and afraid of being left alone in a room, and yet if they felt secure in their environment and had people around them, particularly people they were fond of, you would never have guessed they had anything wrong with them at all. What seems to frighten them is the sheer panic terror itself, which grips them when they feel exposed and unprotected. It is presumably akin to the sensations of a baby on emerging from the mother's womb unless it is immediately wrapped warmly and cradled.

Iris is one of the most gallant people I know. She has suffered from agoraphobia since she was a schoolgirl and yet it has never dimmed the brightness of her spirit, nor has it broken her amazing courage and determination to conquer her fear and live her life to the full. The healing process is very slow and seems to have much to do with the building up of self-confidence and the forming of warm personal relationships. Iris has battled through to victory but it was not always that we were successful in helping people.

Generally we preferred not to talk about success, not because our failure rate was high but because success is such a relative and uncertain commodity. The person who seems to be a success today may be a failure tomorrow. And what in any case is the measure of success? Is it when a man has risen to the top grade in his particular field, or when he has reached rock bottom and has found there the beginnings of self-awareness and understanding? Was Jesus a success during the popularity of his Galilean ministry, or was he a greater success when he hung naked on a criminal's gibbet? Is someone a success when he is well adjusted to society and leads what we call a normal life responding well both to people and to his environment, or is he a success when, like Van Gogh, he seems hopelessly maladjusted and yet creates a new dimension in the world of art? The face of success is so often a mask behind which lurks the fear of failure, or greed for power. Undoubtedly we did have, in the normally accepted sense, considerable success at Pilsdon: people were helped towards greater self-confidence and towards re-establishment in society. But the word 'success' and its underlying concept imply both a judgement and competition — if one man is a success then another man must be a failure — and it was with this judgement and this competitiveness that we were at odds. So we tended to think not in terms of success or unsuccess but rather of non-success — an absence of the whole idea.

Meanwhile, the problems at Pilsdon were all around us. Men and women came because their marriages were breaking or had broken; they came because they were lonely and needed the stimulus and comfort of companionship; they came because they had been let out of prison or a mental hospital and could not deal with their freedom; they came because they were homosexuals and, unable to come to terms with it, felt isolated and alien; they came because they were at war with their parents; they came because they hated school; they came because their friends and relatives needed a break from looking after them; they came because they were poor and needed a holiday; and women came because they were going to have a baby or had just had one and were unprepared for the responsibilities of motherhood. They came by themselves or were brought by parents, friends, or welfare workers. And how did we attempt to deal with this tremendously varied assortment of ailments and troubles? We were often asked what we offered that was not offered by the welfare state and it was sometimes suggested that we were perhaps merely being used by people who were not trying very hard to do anything for themselves.

In reply to this last allegation I think it true to say that the question of merit or demerit, like success or failure, was not part of our thinking. What help we could give was not given because of merit but because of need. We did not weigh people's value and then decide to help those for whom the scales dipped on the side of worth. We helped people simply because they turned to us for help and very often there was no one else to whom they could turn. The welfare state does deal with a great many of the problems that beset men and women and I would not for one moment decry its services but it cannot begin to deal with all of them and one area of special need is for a bridge between an institutional existence such as operates inside a prison or mental hospital and the pressures and demands of life outside and for many people Pilsdon did supply this bridge. What does it feel like to be walking out of the gates of a prison at 7.30 a.m. after two or three years inside that huge encircling wall? It should perhaps be a joyful experience of freedom but more often it is a panic situation. A feeling akin to agoraphobia grips the mind of a man as he stands outside that grim but safe stone womb and steps back again into the wide open spaces of the world. His family has rejected him, his work record is poor or non-existent, and the only friends he has are those with whom he got into trouble last time. Where is he to go? What is he to do? The answer is, make straight for the nearest pub and in a few days or weeks or months there is another disguised cry for help and a return to the bleak safety of those high walls. Another recidivist has been born and it is going to be very difficult for him to break the pattern.

Many of these men, and a few women, came to Pilsdon and sometimes the pattern was either not formed or, in rare instances, it was broken and a person gained a freedom which was not merely physical. One young man was a compulsive car thief but when, after a longish stay at Pilsdon and the formation of a genuine friendship with one of the community members, he found work as a chauffeur and later in a home for the handicapped and acquired a car of his own, the compulsion to steal no longer seemed to operate and he was able to find his place again in a normal social setting.

Loneliness too is not something which can usually be dealt with by the machinery of state organizations and yet it can cause such acute distress that it results in suicide, alcoholism, phobias of every kind, and complete paralysis of the will and any motivation for living. We had many very lonely people living with us: I have mentioned before those men and women who moved amongst us like ghosts of themselves, silent and withdrawn, cutting short every effort at communication and repulsing every attempt to draw them into some joint activity. Their loneliness was both the result and also the cause of their distress. It was the chicken and the egg syndrome and very difficult to resolve. Sometimes the feeling would be attributed to a lack of love in childhood but I came to think this is rarely true just as it stands:

what does seem to be true is that, as with all loving, the kind of love or the quality of love a parent extends to a child must answer the needs of that particular child otherwise he or she does not *feel* loved even though the other children in the same family are not conscious of any lack. However, just allowing these people space within the warmth and security of a family group did much to help them. Living in a community they found themselves almost unconsciously, and without that personal motivated effort which they found so difficult to make, drawn into something which by its very nature and without exerting any undue pressure on them sought, and received, their co-operation.

And although there are such things as Marriage Guidance clinics which give people help with their marital problems often one of the biggest of those problems is that neither partner can sit back, away from the seat of the problem, long enough to get it into any kind of perspective. A young mother with three small children around her all day and a husband expecting a meal as soon as he gets home has no time or space or energy to sort out emotional tangles or deal with marital tensions, and the husband, after a hard day at the office, is also too tired to try. But at Pilsdon we did provide the space and the leisure. Sometimes it was for a husband, sometimes for a wife, and sometimes they came together and the temporary lifting of all the pressures of employment and domestic life gave them the dimension they needed in which to think things out.

However, beyond providing this unpressurized and friendly environment, what did we actually do to help all these people with their multifarious troubles? And the answer is — in the clinical sense, very little. We gave them the space, the support, the security, and within that framework people threaded their own way through their particular jungles and fought their own battles with their special dragons.

There were many props along the way, which were the natural outcome of the way in which we lived. Some people must have been greatly helped by hard physical labour and a tired body at the end of the day, some by working alongside other people and by the satisfaction of doing something with obvious and immediate usefulness. Some needed to learn how to work and concentrate on a job and had to be encouraged to do so. Some needed to talk and be where others were talking; some needed the peace and solitude of the library or chapel. Some needed to find a mother or father figure, and there were plenty to choose from. Some needed appreciation and some needed a hard jolt, which Percy was quite as able to give as any other form of assistance. There was vigour at Pilsdon, the vitality of youthfulness, of a pioneering adventure, and of a healthy, hard, open-air life. There was also beauty — the fields and trees surrounding the house, the Pen, always changing in its patterns of light and shade, the old grey house itself — the large rooms always flower-filled, and the quiet walled garden.

And there was honesty — the total exposure involved in our common life. For some this was unbearable but there is healing in coming face to face with yourself — if you can stand it. And there is healing too in the knowledge that other people know your weaknesses and failings and possibly even your crimes and still manage to go on loving and accepting you. This brings us all a little closer to loving and accepting ourselves and this, in its turn, a little nearer to wholeness.

And a great many people were helped by Percy himself. When they arrived at Pilsdon he usually saw them on the first evening or very soon after and listened while they poured out their difficulties, or perhaps had to wait patiently while they battled with tongue-tying inhibitions, and his kindness and non-judgemental concern, his wide experience of problems of all kinds and the feeling of strength which emanated from him gave them a much-needed sense of security and acceptance. Later they would be able to turn to him again if they needed to and again absorb from him the feeling of calm understanding which lessened their anxiety or their guilt or self-loathing and made them feel more at ease with themselves and the world around them.

But Percy did not encourage constant introspection or too much discussion of problems. Also there were no therapy groups or formal discussions so, apart from these 'interviews' in Percy's study, people were encouraged to throw themselves as actively as possible into the life and work of the community and in this they were helped by everyone who was already doing it and especially by the long-term guests, who would often work alongside a new guest, sometimes talking, sometimes listening, and sometimes just concentrating on work participation. Most of us were pretty well aware the whole time of sensitive and difficult areas both of individual personality and also of relationships and as we were a closely-knit community operating as a single family unit there was always somebody at hand if needed.

This could easily have been a we-them situation and sometimes perhaps it was, or at least felt like it, but we were largely saved from it by the close integration of our life. We were all 'in' something together, working out our problems together and *receiving as well as giving help* (The italics are important). We were all there because we needed Pilsdon in one way or another and together we were creating a 'caring community': many people who had come to receive care stayed to give it and some who had come to give it found they stayed to receive it. And this united us all. In the words of a girl who was on heroin before coming to Pilsdon:

"We work, we laugh, we all have our hang-ups but we have them together. We are a community. We understand each other. We'll come through together."

## X

It was not only in the Pilsdon kitchen that the cowboys featured prominently. They were some of the most picturesque and colourful characters we ever had and there was always a good scattering of them staying with us. They were wayfarers 'of no fixed abode' the most fixed abode of many of them being Her Majesty's Prison, Dorchester, referred to euphemistically as The House of Many Windows or 'The Dorchester'. 'Cowboy' was their own name for themselves but we early adopted it at Pilsdon and it stuck firmly. They were a nomadic tribe wandering from town to town and occasionally doing a spell of hotel portering in the summer, and wintering either in a cell, or under a hedge, or in various reception centres — or at Pilsdon.

Like all tribes the cowboys had their own strict code of honour and behaviour. Generosity among themselves was obligatory and a story Percy liked to tell was of one well-known cowboy who had come to Pilsdon bringing with him, against Percy's express instructions, another friend off the roads and when Percy, true to his word, refused to accept this other cowboy Frank turned out his pockets and gave him everything he had. This kind of generosity was their passport. It made them acceptable anywhere, to any other tribal group.

Many of the cowboys had wandered south from the poorer areas of Glasgow and of other large cities and, after a spell in the army or navy had found themselves restless and unable to settle down to their former way of life. This life had dealt out to most of them a pretty poor hand and alcohol had seen to the rest. They nearly all drank far too much even if they were not actually alcoholics, and if drink did not account for lost homes and hopeless job prospects, then gambling did. They had mostly managed to avoid to a large extent the rigours of a formal education but many of them were exceptionally well-read and knowledgeable.

They referred to each other by nicknames which were as colourful as the characters they represented: Pinhead Murphy, Berry Docherty, Cheeky and

Extra Cheeky, Haggis, Little Caruso (who was very short but had a pair of powerful lungs), Telephone Jock who was always going into telephone kiosks and pretending to ring people up, and One Way Rogers, a merchant seaman who never completed a journey. He would sign on a ship going somewhere and was never seen again by that ship but months later he would sign on another ship going somewhere else and repeat the process. Eventually he ran out of shipping lines and settled in the East End of London. And there was Box Car Riley who travelled round America in freight cars and made quite a name for himself as an international tramp one of his peculiarities being that, when he was drinking everyone had to have a drink with him, but when he was sober everyone was cautioned sternly not to touch 'that awful stuff'. There was the Talking Fish who had lost his teeth very early in life and pursed up his lips when he talked, which he did a great deal, so that he looked like an excited goldfish. And there was the legendary Flying Saucer who earned his splendid title because of his superhuman ability to get round the country faster than any known transport. He acquired the name in Plymouth where a magistrate was trying him on a charge of being drunk and disorderly.

"Is there anything known about the accused?" The magistrate turned to the officiating policeman.

"He was fined ten shillings yesterday for a similar offence in Aberdeen."

"How did he get down here then?"

"By flying saucer!" came the famous reply.

Although we knew many of these cowboys at Pilsdon I had forgotten some of the names so I wrote to Sam and he supplied me with most of them as well as the biographical details. It was when Sam was in the Pilsdon kitchen one night that a strange incident occurred which seemed like long-distance telepathy. He was telling us how he and another cowboy called Taffy Price had been drinking in Bristol one very cold night round about Christmas. It was late and they were looking for some kind of shelter when Taffy suddenly and mysteriously disappeared. He had fallen into a coal bunker. Sam peered down into the blackness.

"Are you all right, Taff?"

"Fine and dandy," came a slightly muffled voice. "Why don't you come down here too?"

But Sam did not fancy the hole so he continued his search alone and finally found the cab of a disused crane in which he curled up and shivered through the night.

Just as Sam was finishing this story there was a peremptory thud on the kitchen door. We knew it must be a stranger because no one who knew Pilsdon well ever knocked on the door. So I went to open it and was astonished to hear a shout from behind me.

"Taffy by God!"

And there was Taffy Price standing in the doorway in an old navy greatcoat, his dishevelled grey hair a bush around his head and his bright eyes taking in every detail of the scene, his stance four-square and slightly aggressive. We were speechless. Taffy had never been to Pilsdon before and his name was hardly out of Sam's mouth when this apparition appeared. When we had recovered we invited him in and sat him down at the kitchen table where he was soon making short work of bacon and eggs and bread and cheese washed down with a large mug of strong tea.

Between them the cowboys had seen the insides of most of the prisons in the country. Their crimes were seldom more than petty theft committed under the influence of alcohol and in hopes of continuing the orgy. Their sentences were usually short and the prison kitchens must often have benefited from their stay as some of them were very good workers and excellent kitchen porters.

Now, with the closing down of so many reception centres, there seem to be fewer cowboys on the road, or perhaps it is just that the particular tribes we knew best have gradually dwindled: many of them have died, some have remarried and opted for a more settled way of life, and a few have almost miraculously turned from alcohol and a life of petty crime and become sober, self-respecting citizens. But, over the years, Pilsdon was at least a temporary home for many of them and we liked to see them come and were sad to see them go. We never knew when this would happen. A cowboy who might have been with us for about four or five months would wake up one fine sunny morning and decide this was the day to take to the roads again, and then and there would shoulder his small pack and be off. But sometimes we could see it coming. There would be an obvious restlessness for some days, more than a touch of irritation, then the air would turn blue over some relatively minor incident, and there would be one man less to lunch that day.

This hasty temperedness was one of the great handicaps of nearly all the cowboys. It was probably caused by the tension mounting inside them when they wanted a drink and also perhaps by a fairly permanent but well hidden sense of inadequacy and failure. But it was a major job handicap because, after only a few weeks, or possibly only a few days working in an hotel somewhere, there would be a flare-up and that particular cowboy would be on the road again.

It was not always due entirely to a congenital quick temper. Hotel working conditions are not usually enviable: kitchens are hot, especially in summer, everyone is overworked, and nobody has any time for the susceptibilities of a down-and-out wayfarer. And many of them were well-read intelligent men who should have been holding down much more responsible jobs and felt the inferiority of their position keenly. It was this susceptibility which was mostly so well hidden by an outward toughness and often by an extrovert joviality of manner which gave no hint of the real isolation which existed within. But they were our friends and I think this friendship did something to alleviate the pain of separateness.

It was easy to be friendly with them: they were so much themselves, so unspoilt by social inhibitions and conventions, by having to keep up some kind of respectable middle-class image, and it is always easiest to like people who are unaffectedly natural. They were true Bohemians living outside normal social behaviour patterns and they had formed their own opinions about men and manners. Many of them had a rich vein of humour; they told marvellously funny stories, and some of them had acquired, perhaps through long solitary hours alone on the roads, an insight and wisdom which was often pithily expressed. I remember one of them saying to me as he rolled his plug of Old Holborn, "You know, there's only the thickness of this tobacco paper between sanity and madness." So true. And so unforgettable.

They were half naive and half cunning, half sad and half funny, like tragi-comic clowns, and who can resist a true clown? They were touchy too and moody and often irritable but they knew they were safe with us, safe from scorn and from censure. There was an affinity between us: we too had chosen an unconventional path and, like them, were living a life that had shed many of the sophistications of society and was simpler and more primitive than most of modern life. Almost unconsciously we understood each other and were relaxed and at home in that understanding.

But although cowboys were a constant feature of Pilsdon life very few real old-fashioned tramps came to our doors. The tramps are different from the cowboys in that they never seem to work at all. Tramping is their occupation and begging their profession. They are always n.f.a. — no fixed abode — whereas the cowboys do sometimes have an address and draw wages. But in the early years at Pilsdon there was an old man who used to visit us as part of his regular beat. We called him Father Christmas and it is rumoured that he died in the severe winter of 1963. He would arrive at about 6.30 in the evening wearing three overcoats. Winter and summer alike he always had his three overcoats, one at least of which was always some kind of military great-coat. He was a wizened little man with straggly, matted grey hair, and the coats came right down to his ankles.

The first time he came I offered him a bath. This was not quite as rude as it sounds. In his case it was a necessity but we always offered wayfarers, when they first arrived, a bath or shower in much the same spirit as in the East in former days the traveller would be offered a basin of water to wash his feet because, after a spell on the roads, it was a luxury to revel in hot water. On this occasion I escorted the old man up to the bathroom and, leaving him there, went to the linen cupboard for a clean towel but on my return I found he had started stripping, with the door wide open, and was clad in only a rather large grey shirt which dangled around his knees. He was just about to take this off as well when I hastily handed him the towel, shut the door, and departed leaving the little grey gnome to his ablutions. That same night Gillian was terrified by the sudden bursting open of her door and there in the darkness stood Father Christmas in his grey shirt but on seeing Gillian's startled face in the light of her torch the door was hastily slammed shut again. As Gillian's bedroom was opposite the bathroom he was obviously heading for the latter but had mistaken the door but it took Gillian some time to recover from this startling apparition in her bedroom at the dead of night.

After supper Father Christmas would sit in the common room reading the paper upside down, then he would be away upstairs to bed and off in the morning before anyone had time to find a job for him. It would be perhaps another six months before we saw him again.

Women seldom seem to take to the wayfaring life although two of the first wayfarers we had were a man and woman called Bill and Blodwen. They had travelled on foot from Cardiff and were exhausted when they arrived. Whatever their relationship was, or was not, it was certainly an uneasy partnership as quarrelling between themselves seemed to take up most of their time. But my chief memory of Blodwen is not related to Bill. It was a Saturday morning and she and I had been given the job of cleaning the church for Sunday. I had one or two things to see to before going down so Blodwen was there when I arrived. Inside the church were various stone gargoyles which might at some time have been brought in from the outside and two of these heads rested on ledges just above the pulpit. Blodwen had gone down armed with a bucket of water, soap, and a scrubbing brush and when I arrived she was standing on the little seat inside the pulpit with the bucket of water poised on an arm of the pulpit itself and engaged in energetically scrubbing the stone faces while singing in a beautiful rich contralto.

"Whatever are you doing, Blodwen?" I asked in amazement.

"Washing their faces for Sunday," came the lilting reply. "I bet they never had it done before."

I betted they hadn't either and wondered how they were enjoying the novel experience.

But if Bill and Blodwen's relationship fell far short of the romantic, Jack and Flo were romanticism personified. She was a little older than him and frail and delicate and dependent, while Jack's life was one of tender devotion to her every need. Sometimes he would go into Bridport, which was six miles away, to do a little shopping and he never came back without some small present for Flo, a little bottle of scent, some beads, or a pretty handkerchief. She never used them but she was pleased with these tokens of his devotion. But Flo died a short time after they had stayed with us and then Jack's life fell apart. He had several heart attacks and he too died not very long after her.

Occasionally a woman would be on the road by herself but this was a rare occurrence, and she was a loner belonging to no wayfaring tribe, outcast, pathetic, and usually a little mad.

The cowboys were rarely mad: it was often their sense and sanity which gave Pilsdon much of its stability. It is true they were often unreliable and irresponsible and their cowboy game was pure fantasy but it was all offset by an intelligence and humour which mostly kept them free from psychotic unreality. When they were hauled before the magistrates they preferred prison to the psychiatric wing of a hospital, and it suited them better.

But the romantic lure of life on the roads is not, in reality, quite as romantic as it sometimes seems to the bored resident of suburbia or the young anarchist. There is a certain freedom from the claims and demands of society but it too often turns out to be a freedom to be cold, to be hungry, to be caked in mud from head to foot, to be wet through, to be despised, to be lonely. Many of the cowboys we knew at Pilsdon have now died. Longevity is not one of their attributes. Exposure, alcohol, poor food, and lack of proper sleep take a heavy toll: their chests are wheezy, their stomachs ulcerous, and very few of them seem to live much beyond sixty. Some of them were ill at Pilsdon, or at nearby hospitals where we could visit them. And we even attended one or two funerals. But most of them died in an unknown hovel and were buried in unknown graves.

Fred was one of the few who had a better send-off. When he died in Boscombe in 1965 his landlady got into touch with us and six of us went, on a very cold snowy day, to Boscombe cemetery. When we arrived at the small cemetery chapel there were no other mourners but a Presbyterian minister was awaiting the arrival of the hearse. Much to his astonishment we begged to be allowed to sing Fred's favourite hymn. At first he tried to parry our enthusiasm by pointing out that there was no hymn book, but our insistence won the day. A musty hymnal was fished out from a dingy corner and I opened up the harmonium. So Fred was played in to his funeral and played out again and, in between, six good strong voices gave a pretty fair, memorized rendering of Crimond. During the service the landlord and a friend came to pay their last respects but Fred was the youngest of a family of thirteen some of whom were probably still alive. It was not their fault they were not there. Their brother had cut himself off from them: the wayfaring life knows no domestic ties or responsibilities and so it finishes with no fanfare or public proclamation.

Fred had never been married but many of the cowboys had wives and children whom they never saw. They were mostly lacking in any bitterness or resentment about this: they knew they had deserved the rejection of their families and they accepted it as inevitable, but sometimes with a slightly wistful nostalgia. A few of them, while they were in the family setting of Pilsdon, recontacted mothers or sisters or brothers — never wives — but it was generally a short-lived and abortive undertaking. They had turned their backs on all this and for many of them the doors of home had forever been shut in their faces. And yet it may have been that some of their families yearned over them far more than they ever realized.

They had mostly a slightly old-fashioned courtesy towards women and a tenderness towards small children. I remember one night when a friend and I were sitting talking in the kitchen, the door opened and a tall, rather dishevelled man stood smiling apologetically in the doorway. He was very drunk but he lurched forwards and bowed gallantly over our hands, hiccuping gently and trying rather vainly to explain his sudden and unexpected appearance. He wanted to stay the night and when told that the rules of the house only permitted him, in his inebriated state, a bed in the barn outside, he confessed shyly that he was a little afraid of the 'wee mooses'. We christened him Drunken Duncan and remember him still for his gentle quixotic courtesy.

There were some men who, although not cowboys themselves, seemed loosely connected with them and lived on the fringes of their domains. Danny first came to Pilsdon in 1959. He had a regular job erecting television pylons but he seemed to know and be known by many of the cowboys. He met them in pubs and later on the connection was often Pilsdon. But although Danny was in regular employment he seemed to be able to work to suit himself and when his 'ulcer' was bad after a spell of heavy drinking, or at holiday time, he would make his way to Pilsdon and sit on the top of our roof pegging in slates that had fallen off in the high gales. He always worked in his shirt sleeves however bleak and bitter the weather and the Pilsdon roof owes its survival to his labours. His own survival was due to Bisodol. He was a walking advertisement for it and on his arrival one day at tea-time was presented with Bisodol sandwiches.

He had a great facility for getting himself into awkward situations some of which nearly landed him in serious trouble. On one occasion, when we had just finished tea, there was a knock at the door and I opened it to find three men in the hallway.

"Could we speak to Danny Byrne?"

"Three friends to see you, Danny," I sang out cheerfully into the crowded common room only to be motioned outside quickly by one of the men.

"We're the CID," he whispered.

I shut the door hastily and showed them into the library while I went to inform Danny of the identity of his 'friends'.

They had come to interview him because there had been a murder a few days before in the village where Danny had been staying just prior to coming to Pilsdon, and as he had been known to leave the village shortly after the crime had been committed he was naturally one of the suspects. So I went into the library with Danny and testified to his good name and after he had answered all their questions and I had written out a statement and signed it they were satisfied and they shook hands with both of us and the matter was dropped. But it was the kind of thing that happened to Danny. In all innocence he seemed to attract misfortune.

He came from Southern Ireland and had been trained as a shoe-maker and was one of the few who followed the fortunes of the community and visited it loyally for the whole of the twenty years of which I am writing. And still does.

If I have mentioned some names and omitted others it is not because they were necessarily better known to us or figured more prominently in the life of Pilsdon but because they happen to illustrate some point I wish to make and if I were to personalize them all this would be a book about nothing but cowboys. Nevertheless I have given them space to themselves because they were a race apart, as distinctive as the true travelling people, and it may well be that there will soon not be many of them left.

## XI

Perhaps some of the people who responded most readily and were most permanently affected by a stay at Pilsdon were the many teenagers, or slightly older, who came to us because they felt life to be meaningless or oppressive. Many of them were rebelling against formal upbringings and disciplines, against the regimen of schools, against conventional parents, against work expectations and, from whatever background they had originally come, against class barriers and class traditions. And this almost total rejection of everything around them had resulted in a state of near-paralysis, depression, or apparent inadequacy. They had no directives, no purpose, and very little faith in anything. So there was often drug addiction, suicide attempts (or sometimes, tragically, the real thing), and aggressive or criminal tendencies.

The parents were often not to blame in all this. They were hurt, bewildered, uncomprehending, and sometimes almost distraught. They loved their children and had brought them up to the best of their ability. They had tried to pass on to them their own values and codes of behaviour and their children seemed to be so wilful in their disregard of everything they had so painstakingly inculcated in them. Where had they gone wrong? What had happened?

Nothing had gone wrong. It was just that they were finding it very difficult to understand the new world in which their children were growing up and feeling their way. Everything was changing. There was a revolution in values and the young were swept up into it. There were new attitudes to everything, new clothes, new hair styles, new ways of walking and talking, new ideas about sex, about love and all relationships. And the new was sometimes as confusing for the young as it was for their parents, the difference being that they were prepared to step forward while some of the parents were back-pedalling as fast as they could go.

Much of this was in the 1960s and early seventies. By now things have changed again. Many parents have by this time adopted some of the fashions and life-style of their children. Possibly even more so. It is often the children now who are worried about their parents because the parents cannot do the new things with quite the same flair as their children and behave in a way which belongs neither to the old nor to the new, emergent, sense of values, one of these being an emotional honesty which sometimes looks like rudeness.

Pilsdon was always full of these young men and women, some of them almost boys and girls. Most of them strummed guitars, hated school, wore unisex jeans frayed around the bottom, read Tolkien and Hermann Hesse, went to pop festivals, made plans for hitch-hiking across Europe, and had mostly lived on or near the fringes of the drug scene. And what did they find at Pilsdon to attract them? What drew them there and why did they stay?

One of the things they found at Pilsdon was the opportunity just to be themselves without the pressures of schoolteachers, parents, or employers, and this freedom often resulted in a growing awareness of themselves and of what they wanted to do or be. It was easier for us than for their parents to disregard some of their oddities of behaviour or clothing. They were not our own children so we were not concerned with our own image mirrored in them and however liberal and enlightened we may think we are none of us are quite immune to this where our own families are concerned. I speak as a parent.

At Pilsdon too they seemed to forget about their quarrel with adults, and the generation gap. Perhaps it was partly because we all did the same work and shared the same kind of life. It was a return to a more tribal form of existence where the young and old worked and played together, followed the same pattern of living and shared the same experiences. Also, in order to give the community full cohesion there was an interdependence between all groups so that the younger people felt as much an integral part of the whole as did the older ones — perhaps sometimes more so as there were always so many of them. The average age at Pilsdon was often well below the middle. And in such a cohesive situation things like long hair and ragged jeans ceased to be divisive and, if noticed at all, were a subject for frivolous comment rather than disapproval. We had the great advantage of living away from most conventional situations so that the conventional manners and the conventional clothes which they mostly disliked were never needed.

They also enjoyed the exposure to so many different experiences of life, the excitement of meeting people from such varied backgrounds. They almost all made friends amongst the cowboys and listened avidly to their tales of life on the roads. They found the world was bigger than they had thought and there was more to it than doing a dull routine job from 9 to 5. Some of them found a renewed interest in an educational process which they had scorned, and returned to colleges, or entered them, or took O and A levels by correspondence. Many decided, after seeing the very real suffering of so many people, that they wanted to help in some kind of way and took jobs in homes for the handicapped, or took a training in social welfare work. Here is what one girl writes about her experiences of Pilsdon.

At Pilsdon, instead of dropping out, you drop in. Living there is a shared secret. Ambitions tend towards hopes for a good potato crop. Luxury is, (or was for me at my 18th birthday dinner), mushrooms in the spaghetti sauce. Strange things become invested with importance — and one's perception of almost everything is radically and inevitably changed.

I was lucky to be raw enough to believe in magic. Unlike others, who were broken and busted up inside, whose versions of reality had been stamped and trodden into them through prison, alcoholism, hospitalization and drugs, I came receptive as an empty bucket. Embarrassingly shy, perhaps, and spoilt, unused to sharing, I had made little social headway in the normal run of things. An awkward adolescent who despised the pantomime of ritual chit-chat, (my mother at one point despaired into labelling me a social misfit), who refused dourly to conform to the politics of behaviour — imagine my delight at dropping in; at discovering a highly organized and successful structure which broke all the rules; at sharing the secret.

Briefly, the importance of Pilsdon is that it lets people be. Despite the never-ending list of tasks which need to be done, and done well, to keep the structure solid, there is so much space. Acceptance is probably the first lesson, and I feel ashamed, even now, that some of my closest friends are people whom on first meeting seemed to have nothing in common with me, nothing to offer. If not forced into the closest of proximities, forced to live and work together, I would have been arrogantly dismissive and would have missed out on a great deal. With acceptance comes tolerance and, as an only child, I had previously needed to tolerate very little. I've been privileged all my life, lucky and loved — it's only in hearing the nightmares of others, and seeing them cope with their history, learning to function at their own pace, breathing the reality of Pilsdon (which makes the rest of the world seem ludicrously unreal) that someone like me can learn about perspective and I feel, ten years later, very thankful at having had what I consider to be a unique education.

Everyone has a story to tell, and it's all valid. It's also quite normal at Pilsdon for a bishop to be doing the washing up with a tramp. The meaning of work has little to do with money or personal gain. The lowliest chores can be rewarding when one realizes that some thirty other people are benefiting from it, (a roomful of people sighing with delight over their strawberries and cream means a hell of a lot when it's you who picked the strawberries).

I lived at Pilsdon for about two years and I think I did begin to understand it — it takes a while to peel away the layers, it can't be done over a visit for tea. Even now I don't profess to know how or why, only that it is and that it should be. I suffer from a tendency to over-analyse and sharing one's days with people labelled 'sick' did sometimes make me feel 'sick' too. That, and the womb-like security, (which can only be temporary if Pilsdon is to succeed in helping individuals to reconstruct their lives and reintegrate with society) which lulls one into false hopes of life and love, which can be shattered on impact with the outside world, are the negative aspects of life in the community. When you're closeted in a fairytale which is as real as anything ever will be, it can become a puzzle too deep to unravel and that's probably why I, like many others before and since, keep coming back — to take another shot at figuring it all out, to share the secret a little bit more.

Some of these young people elected to stay near us and found work in the immediate vicinity of Pilsdon as farm workers or gardeners or in small local factories. Some even joined the community and for many years we had the stimulus and vision provided by lively young community members. Miles was one of these. He joined us in 1974. He was a student architect who had decided to give up academic training in favour of something more practical and he quickly found an empathy with Pilsdon. Less confident inside than he appears on the outside, Miles has a deep, though mostly hidden, need for appreciation and affection. He also has a wide range of talents and abilities and the energy to apply them so that his own needs met an answering response in the needs of Pilsdon. He became a vital and enthusiastic part of everything that happened there. He planned and, with help, built what we called our 'theatre', converting it from an outside barn so that it had a stage and a minstrel's gallery. He also planned and organized and worked on the conversion of an outside shed into the craft room with display shelves and generous working surfaces. He sang bass in the choir, did endless chauffeuring, threw pots in the pottery, and even found time to belong to a dramatic society in Bridport. And in addition to all this, whenever anything went wrong with the electricity or a door fell off its hinges, or a sock was tangled up in the works of the washing machine, we ran for Miles.

Maralyn was also a community member at this time. She had been a teacher but found herself out of sympathy with the disciplines and regimen of school life. Again, like Miles, her nature found an answering chord in the community existence of Pilsdon. She relates easily and well to people, never brushing them aside and always giving them her full attention. This is invaluable in a busy working community where time is often at a premium, and Maralyn had plenty of scope for its full exercise especially as it is combined in her with an infectious sense of humour. Also she is committed to a belief in new age doctrines and philosophies, to a spiritual quest which finds itself most at home in a community setting where togetherness is both an ideal and a practical experience. But after a time both Maralyn and Miles began to feel that there was not enough challenge for them at Pilsdon. The first exciting pioneering days were over when they arrived and they came in to a more settled community existence with most of the guide-lines already mapped out and I think they would have liked some of the experiences we had been through. They would also have liked more responsibility for the running of Pilsdon and we older community members perhaps kept too tight a hold on the main structures of the community life. It is always difficult to know how, and when, to delegate authority. It is difficult to entrust what has been so carefully and painstakingly built up into the hands of others and yet, if this is not done, the life stream eventually dries up.

Peter and Margareta were also young community members. They came to us already married but without a family and lived for a time in the first of the converted loose boxes. It was a tiny enough room for a married couple to share: the total area cannot have been more than about nine feet square. But the loose boxes were cosy inside. They had stable doors, in front of which most of the inhabitants hung heavy curtains as draught excluders, but they backed onto a solid stone wall and they could be made quite hot, even stuffy, with the aid of an oil stove. Their chief disadvantage, being situated close to the animals, was mice — or were they rats? Most people did not investigate but one man regularly threw his shoe every night in the direction from which the scuffling noises came. Fortunately they were more a sound than a presence but the sound was intimidating enough.

Peter had wanted to become a clergyman but was refused training by the advisory council of the church so we asked them if they would like to join us and Peter and Margareta lived at Pilsdon for nearly two years giving generously to it of their love and their friendliness and sense of fun. But after their first baby, Heidi, was born they moved down to live at the cottage and, with the emergence of their own family existence, life at Pilsdon became less satisfactory for them and they left to set up their own home in Derbyshire.

Ruth and Trevor stayed with us longer. They had met when they were both living at Lee Abbey, a much larger community than Pilsdon near Lynton in North Devon. But they were married at Pilsdon and became community members.

They had much to give Pilsdon. Ruth was a trained cook-caterer and Trevor a partially trained musician with a love for the outdoors which quickly found satisfaction in full-time work in the huge vegetable garden. But it was their unaffected friendliness which was their best contribution to the life of the community. People were instinctively drawn to them and the places where they lived; first a room in the cottage and then the annexe became a sort of Pilsdon within Pilsdon. Many people poured out their troubles on the wide sofa or stayed up long after the lights of the house had gone out to discuss life and its problems with Ruth and Trevor. They were always warmly welcoming and the spirit of Pilsdon was nowhere more in evidence than in the rooms which they made their home.

But they too left Pilsdon after a few years, their departure perhaps hastened by the birth of two children, Robert and Nicola, and the ensuing difficulties of life within the confined limitations of a community.

Pilsdon was not at that time well suited to the needs of small family units within the larger community structure. There was always the pull both ways, between the attention needed by the smaller unity and the time and energy given to the whole. The wife found that her husband belonged to everybody, or vice versa, but mostly the first way round if the wife was also the mother of a small family. Meals being communal she missed the cosy family gathering around the table over which she presided and at which she exercised some of her maternal functions. She found she had lost some of her role as wife and mother and yet she was often too tired, physically and emotionally by her children, to be able to throw herself into the activities of the community.

Unlike the kibbutzim in Israel we had not developed a pattern of equal comradeship between men and women with the children being looked after communally. Although the children were an indispensable part of the whole structure of Pilsdon and were present with us at nearly all meals and shared with us the use of all the public rooms, they were still looked after within their own families and still claimed most of the time and attention of their mothers. So it was always a slightly uneasy situation and there was always a danger of the marriage coming unstuck. And this was a pity because the young families gave Pilsdon a warm, homely feeling and a sense of things being natural and normal which the community badly needed.

So these young community members were vital to the growth of Pilsdon and they drew other young people easily and naturally into its orbit. Ruth, our daughter, was one of Pilsdon's young people. She grew up in it and when she was older attended some of our community meetings. She shared in every aspect of our life and we did not shield her, by dishonesty or by silence, from a knowledge of the problems and traumas which were all around us. Perhaps it was partly this feeling of sharing in the complexities of an adult world which smoothed the path for her into her own adulthood and obviated many of the difficulties which so many people seem to experience in adolescence. Ruth loved Pilsdon and, even after her marriage she and Mike kept strong links with it and came back often with their family, to be part of it again.

But bringing up a child in a community had its own peculiar problems not the least being that we were bringing up our child in public under the scrutiny of many pairs of eyes and it is axiomatic that everyone thinks they can bring up a child better than its parents and I was always conscious of possible censorship.

Percy too suddenly found himself, almost overnight, in a new position of authority over people's lives and this necessarily included the life of his daughter. Like everyone else she was subject to the Pilsdon disciplines. She no longer had any meals in private with the family and family outings became a thing of the past. She still had her pony which we had brought with us from Hawkchurch, and every day after school she went for a ride round the lanes closely followed by Smog, our border collie. But this was almost the only link with the life which she had known before. Existence underwent, for all of us, a fairly dramatic change and it was to Ruth's credit that she not only survived but learnt from it and contributed a great deal to the new way of living by her ready friendship, her courage, and her enjoyment of life.

It was at Pilsdon that Ruth met, and later married, Mike Thurgur now best known for an international squash reputation. He had spent the summer at the community deciding what to do after taking a history degree at Exeter University and it was in the Pilsdon library in the evening, where Mike studied and Ruth did her prep, that their friendship began. At first it was a source of embarrassment to both of them, to Mike because Ruth was still a schoolgirl, and to Ruth because she was still ordered to bed in the evening like a child. But in spite of the difficulties their relationship grew and deepened and on March 27th 1967 they were married in the tiny church at Pilsdon.

Many other men and women have been married at Pilsdon and it is the perfect setting — the beauty and spaciousness of the large rooms and wide lawns, the tiny church packed to the doors and overflowing with flowers, the home catering, and the warmth of friendliness — these give to the occasion a sincerity which is deeply moving and full of joy. I have just recently been back to Pilsdon for a wedding and everything was the same, the same beauty, the same warmth, the same sincerity, the same joy.

So Ruth went to her own home. She had been eleven when we had first uprooted her from the cosy family life at Hawkchurch and transplanted her into a community setting, and now she was nineteen and ready to move back again into the kind of world from which she had been taken ten years before. She had not, like a kibbutz child, been reared wholly in community and I have often been asked whether she was happy at Pilsdon, whether she suffered from the change and missed some of the more intimate aspects of family existence. And here I will let her speak for herself. These are her own words exactly as she wrote them for me.

I am often asked how it felt being brought up in a community and how it has influenced my life. And I always answer without reservation that it was an upbringing for which I shall be eternally grateful. I was surrounded by rich experiences, and my eyes were opened to a breadth of life which few teenagers can experience.

My parents were very aware of the possible dangers involved in bringing me up in such an exposed environment and were always careful to maintain the feeling of a 'family' and I don't remember feeling in any way second place in their priorities. My needs were always uppermost in their minds and consequently I grew up with a strong sense of security.

Of course there were moments when living with thirty people was difficult, notably at 5 p.m. after a long day at school when expected to tell numerous people in turn what I had or hadn't learnt that day! There are also inevitable petty conflicts in any community life but, Pilsdon being in such an idyllic setting, I was able to escape for my moments of solitude either on foot or on my pony, to the surrounding hills.

My school life and the one I led at Pilsdon were always pretty divorced from each other; it was almost as if I acted two roles. I had close friends at school, but I didn't really lead the kind of life outside school that most of my teenage friends did, but this didn't seem to matter, nor did I feel isolated or unable to communicate with them.

In spite of my intense love of Pilsdon and the profound effect it has had on so much of my thinking, by the time I was 19 I had started to feel slightly stifled by it and desperately needed to taste the so-called 'normal life'. So therefore when I married Mike I needed to experience living in a little house, just the two of us, with my own pots and pans.

Since then I have seen our lives revolving round the circle and after a few years of married life we started to have students living with us and more and more our home has become a place where people can come and be with us for whatever reason. Now there is a constant flow of students and friends in our home whether it is to watch 'Match of the Day', play with the children, or to pour out their sorrows; surely Pilsdon must have given us the capacity to create a little community in our own home, and for me this is a good compromise situation between the commitment to total community which is a very hard one, and living with your own small select group. I like to feel that people are welcome to join in the life of our home and take us as they find us.

I shall cherish all my life the friendships I have made with so many wonderful people at Pilsdon.

The making of relationships so often seems to be the pivot on which normality hangs. But close relationships were not always easy at Pilsdon: they were often slightly strained. There was very little privacy: nobody had his own room except the community members and even some of those shared part of the time, and there was a natural and inevitable curiosity about everyone's doings which still further limited any kind of private existence. Living as we did in one large group, our life was almost totally exposed to the public gaze. It was difficult for two people even to go for a walk together without somebody noticing and remarking on it. When the people staying with us had cars of their own it was easier for them to get away and be alone but otherwise it was virtually impossible except for very short periods of time. The curiosity was not usually malicious or disapproving, unless there was some jealousy involved, but even at its most innocuous it was an intrusion into people's personal lives.

And there were some rather sad young people, very often girls, who stood a little wistfully, and sometimes angrily, on the edges of the young groups, who wore slightly old-fashioned clothes, and always travelled respectably in trains, who had no boy-friends and were frightened of sex.

Some of these were intensely frustrated and very unhappy. Some had taken to wrist-slashing which seemed to give them temporary relief, a kind of masturbation, but was difficult for us to know how to deal with. I remember one girl asking for my help at about ten minutes to eleven one night, just before the lights were due to go out. She had cut her arm quite deeply with a razor and was bleeding profusely. My first thought was to ring a doctor but she assured me she had done it many times before and would be quite all right if I just bandaged her up. So I did the best I could but lay awake for a long time worrying as to whether I had bandaged her too tightly or not tightly enough. She, on the other hand, slept well: the tension had all gone out of her.

And yet, paradoxically, Pilsdon was an easy place to make friends and certainly offered people the opportunity for friendships both platonic and sexual. Sometimes they were hothouse plants which withered when removed from the surroundings which had propagated them, but many of these relationships grew and deepened and stood the strain of being transplanted into less fertile soil. A great many men and women made friendships at Pilsdon which have survived all the twists and turns of fortune and are still a vital part of their lives. And all Pilsdonians greet each other like long lost friends however infrequently they meet.

In addition to all these young people there were always children at Pilsdon. Often, especially in the summer, there would be as many as seven or eight, sometimes only two or three, but Pilsdon would have been unthinkable without them. Our own grandchildren Becky and Justin, were often with us. They loved Pilsdon — the people, the space, the freedom.

At first many of the children came to stay without their parents. They came because a family break-up was in progress or because their mother was too ill to look after them or because they were already in care and were transferred to Pilsdon. Two small coloured boys came because their mother was doing a graduate course at London university, and one family came because their father was in prison and their mother had no home in which to look after them.

In February 1960 a woman telephoned Pilsdon. She was distraught and incoherent — would someone please just go and sit with her for an hour? Living with her two children in a cottage which was dark and dank she had become physically ill and emotionally defeated. So we answered her cry for help. The children, aged ten and eight, were moved to our cottage where Margaret looked after them for a month while the mother went into hospital for a week and then joined us at Pilsdon subsequently returning to her own cottage with her children after a working party from the community had repaired and redecorated it.

This was the kind of emergency with which we were sometimes faced. Often there would be three or four children at the cottage at the same time, some of them fairly severely disturbed by break-up or neglect or violence in the family and Margaret's task was no sinecure. But although they lived down at the cottage with Margaret looking after them, the children were still very much a part of the community. If they were old enough they went to school at Marshwood, the nearest village. There was a school bus which collected them and returned them in the afternoon, and always they had tea with us, sitting on the window-sill dangling their little legs and eyeing us all with tentative friendliness.

If they were below school age they were taken out for walks in the afternoon by someone from the house. This gave Margaret a few hours' break and also meant that everyone had the chance to get to know the children. But entertaining children is not everybody's idea of fun and some people found the afternoon outings more of a trial than a delight. But some of the men, especially those who were fathers themselves and were separated from their own children, would have them beside them while they worked, letting them help with whatever was going on, and one rather taciturn, rough-looking man would sit for hours with a little girl on his knee crooning to her and telling her stories. Some people seem able to talk easily and naturally to children when they are completely unable to communicate with adults, and for these people especially the children were the happiest part of Pilsdon.

The cottage was not attached to the house but stood two fields away in a triangle of grass where the road divided to go to Bridport or to come on to the manor house. A tiny stream skirted the road, which was a very narrow country lane, and this steam was both a hazard and a delight for the cottage dwellers. The triangular patch of grass on which the cottage stood was a fair size and had its own garden which was lovingly tended by Les who lived at Pilsdon for so many years that nobody could remember it without him. In later years he looked after all the cottage mothers in turn. We laughingly referred to them as his 'wives' but he called them all 'gals' so that he became known as Les 'boy'. He is still at Pilsdon, still looking after the cottage garden, still treasuring his collection of stamps, still building up the common room fire in winter, and still ready with wisecracks such as "Always be sincere even if you don't meant it." This text used to hang above his bed together with numerous photographs of his Pilsdon friends in home-made frames which he spent his evenings making down at the cottage when he was baby-sitting.

Later, when Margaret came to live at the main house, the cottage remained a place for children but they then came with their mothers, or with both parents, and the families lived down at the cottage together. It was often shared by two families as it was a sizeable building. Originally it had probably been two farm cottages and had four rooms upstairs and three downstairs together with a junk room and tiny bath-room and back kitchen. I think some of the mothers felt rather isolated and lonely down there and also, as the catering was done in bulk from the house, they were sometimes frustrated by not being able to order just what food their children were accustomed to having. But other mothers enjoyed being at the cottage and were hospitable. People used to drift across to the cottage for a chat or a change of scenery, and sometimes to unburden their troubles and enjoy a secret cup of coffee when they were supposed to be hard at work. Also, as the cottage was on the lane leading to the house, cowboys often called there while they tried to pluck up the courage to return and face the community after a spell away either on the roads or in prison. And people also called there last when they were leaving, sometimes in sadness, and occasionally in anger.

So there were always children around us, cooking with us in the kitchen and plastering the table with dough, romping on the lawn, falling into the pond — every Pilsdon child did this at least once — watching the milking with fascinated eyes, stroking the calves, riding their tricycles round the courtyard, swinging on the gates and paddling in the stream. They went with us to the beach in the summer, and on picnics, and occasionally an energetic person would take them up on the Pen to fly their kites.

## XII

In *Alternative Communities* published by The Teachers it states: 'We find that successful communities which manage to last are usually religious or strongly idealistic and/or have strong leadership.' Well Pilsdon had all three but there are many factors which contribute to the strength, or weakness, of any given community and one of them, at Pilsdon, was the character, abilities, and undeviating loyalty of its community members some of whom, the younger ones, I have written about already. No story of Pilsdon would be complete, or recognizable to those who know it, without specific mention of them and if I here include a few lightly sketched portraits it may also serve to give an insight into the sort of people who are attracted to community life as well as how these particular men and women contributed to the growth and survival of Pilsdon.

Gillian was with us right from the beginning. Her home was at Hawkchurch where Percy was Rector before starting on the Pilsdon venture, so we knew her before we had even heard of Pilsdon and she was a part of it from the start. Without Gillian the community might never have been actualized and would certainly never have grown so strong and self-reliant. She was, in some ways, the epitome of both inner and outer strength, although hidden behind the apparent strength was a lack of self-confidence stemming from childhood. Also, in her, Percy had found someone with a similar outlook and similar reactions to many things so that they were able easily and naturally to share much of Pilsdon's life and ethos.

Pilsdon suited Gillian's natural talents and abilities well and she gave of them freely. She had been brought up in a large country house with a farm attached and later had travelled extensively in Australia and New Zealand with a friend who is now Myrtle Simpson and the author of several travel books. They made their way cooking for farmers on huge ranches and all this experience together with an intelligent and enquiring mind and keen powers of observation had given her a wealth of knowledge about all domestic matters, including large-scale cooking and catering, and most things connected with country life, all of which was invaluable at Pilsdon.

So it was Gillian who ran the Pilsdon herd which generally consisted of about eight or ten cows and calves. She catered for the whole community and was an excellent and economical cook with a flair for *haute cuisine*. She was also responsible for the growing of the soft fruit of which there was always an abundant supply, and after high blood pressure had virtually put a stop to Evelyn's activities in the flower garden Gill took over the running of it and worked in it tirelessly — although no mention of Gill and the garden would be complete without telling of Seamus who, after years of wayfaring, found a niche at Pilsdon and worked in the garden from morning till night every day of the week for many years and is working there still. He could always be found there, digging, weeding, tying up plants and bedding them out, and had a way not only with flowers but also with young people and was loved by them.

Gill too was good at all crafts. In the autumn she was busy with needle and thread and after Christmas all her friends and relatives were clad in the latest trendy waistcoats or jackets. She could throw a pot but seldom had the time to do so, and she had her own spinning wheel. People loved to watch her spinning in the evening in the common room and the gentle whirring sound gave the rather elegant room almost the air of a Gaelic cottage. And when visitors arrived on a sunny day they would as likely as not see Gill sitting outside in the courtyard with her back to the milking parlour making large baskets out of reeds from her family home in Hawkchurch. By training she was the complete countrywoman but by nature she was neither naive nor unsophisticated but had a keen intelligence, a taste for repartee, and a sometimes devastating wit.

But one of Gillian's finest contributions to the life at Pilsdon was the way she enjoyed, or appeared to enjoy, working alongside people and while they worked together Gill listened to their troubles and offered good, common-sense advice. As she was so seldom lazy, stupid, or ignorant herself she was often critical of imperfections in others (she was born under Virgo and one rather amusing astrological book we once read said that when Virgos got to heaven they would find even the angels singing flat) but she had a very real care and concern for people, a deep loyalty, and a great kindness which was unsparing if anyone needed her help. A great many people will be forever grateful to Gill for her generous and unfailing support in all their troubles.

Sidney arrived next. He came with a friend in 1959 to stay for a fortnight and has been at Pilsdon ever since as a full community member. He is spastic though not cripplingly so but when he came to us he was beginning to despair of finding any niche for himself where he could lead a relatively normal life and where his ability to work would be accepted and put to use. He has brothers and sisters and they are a close-knit family but he did not want to be a burden on any of them or to spend his life constantly on the move from one to the other. Neither did he want to become a permanent inmate of a Cheshire home where he felt he would be treated too much as an invalid. He wanted what everyone is now coming to realize the disabled need, a full and satisfying life. So, for Sidney, Pilsdon became the answer. Here he could look after the pigs and poultry which he was well qualified to do being a farmer's son and, in addition, we soon found that he was an outstandingly good guest master and nearly all visitors who came to Pilsdon were, for many years, shown round by Sidney. Once people had recovered from their initial shock at his appearance and had learnt to allow for the slight impediment in his speech they found that his quick intelligence, his wide knowledge, his humour and his wisdom made a guided tour by him a revelation in more ways than one. It not only gave them an insight into the purpose and activities of Pilsdon but also gave them a new understanding of what it means to be born spastic. Many of them felt ashamed they had previously dismissed people with this disability as mentally retarded and they very soon realized that far from this being the case Sidney is highly intelligent and a great reader, his favourite subjects being history and political biographies. In some ways he was always more in touch with the world than any of us.

Sidney is an optimist too and a fighter. Many guests who stayed at Pilsdon were at least temporarily shamed out of their paralysing self-pity by seeing the philosophical acceptance and courage of a man who in some ways had so much less in life than they had themselves. Every move that Sidney makes takes a deliberate concentrated energy and the occasional involuntary spasm of the muscles must be a constant trial especially at meal times. And yet, for many years, he fed the pigs, refusing help with the heavy buckets, and forced the reluctant squealing gilts into the weighing machine, looked after the hens, collected the eggs and washed them for sale, an operation which required a delicacy of handling which even normal hands often found difficult. And when, in the winter of 1977, Sidney found himself rapidly becoming paralysed and was taken to the neurological department of Southampton hospital where they operated on his spine, he fought his way back from near-paralysis to almost his accustomed independence by sheer grit and force of will power. Every day he fought for greater mobility, never succumbing to the temptation to resign himself to wheel-chair invalidism, taking his courage in both hands and forcing his legs to carry him to the house, first with a stick and then unaided, and forcing his hands to movements of increasing dexterity. Several times in the first few weeks he almost lost that courage and whispered to me: "It seems so unjust that I should have been put back to square one and have to start all over again," but this mood was never allowed to get a real grip on his spirit. Every day he had some slight new improvement to report so that by now we have almost forgotten that only three years ago we were afraid we were going to lose him.

Perhaps there were some people at Pilsdon whom Sidney helped more than anyone else could have done. Disabled himself he gave everyone courage. "Is Sid still with you?" is usually the first question anyone asks when they contact Pilsdon or return to it after a long absence. This is possibly his best and most enduring tribute.

And here, because I am speaking of gallantry, I must mention Granny and Ruth. Granny as we all came to call her must have had something of Don Quixote in her make up. She was an elderly widow living with her unmarried daughter, Ruth, in Worcestershire and, fired with enthusiasm for an untried but seemingly Utopian existence, they joined Pilsdon as community members in April 1959. They both loved gardening and Ruth looked after the flower garden while Granny, too old for most of the more active employments, arranged the flowers around the house and, following no school of floral arrangement, Constance Spry or any other, made them beautiful because she loved them. Ruth also helped with the cooking and Granny was an assiduous letter-writer who also wrote poetry and probably other things as well. She was an old-fashioned gentlewoman, cultured, gracious, and a little imperious. Ruth was less sure of herself and often anxious and burdened but she had great warmth of heart and a delightful puckish sense of humour. However, Uoptias are impossible dreams and Pilsdon was very far from being an ideal place so gradually both Granny and Ruth came to feel it was not quite what they had hoped it would be, and they left to settle again in their beloved border country. But Granny was 73 and it had been a heroic adventure.

Margaret came to us from Canada, not quite straight from there, but Toronto was her home town. She had come to England in 1950 and had taught at the Violet Melchett School in London, a training college for nursery teachers. We met her in Hawkchurch where she was staying on holiday with friends, and when she heard about the possibility of Pilsdon and that it would include children she decided, for better or for worse, to throw in her hand with us. So she joined the community in 1959 and at first lived down at the cottage where she looked after children who were in temporary need of care. Sometimes there would be three or four children at the cottage at the same time and as some of them were fairly severely disturbed by the break-up of a marriage or by violence in the home, Margaret's job was no sinecure although there were the rewards and compensations there always are in looking after children. And also the humour. One morning she found a little red-head sitting on a very wet sheet and roundly declaring, "I dunno who done it but 'twasn't me." This same plump piece of mischief regularly ran away from anyone who enticed him out for a walk in the afternoon, was regularly hauled over the coals, and just as regularly grinned his way back into everyone's affection.

In the early days when Margaret was down there we had a field telephone system between the house and cottage which operated with a greater or lesser, mostly lesser, degree of efficiency. But even with this means of communication there was a certain sense of isolation about living down there away from the main scene of communal activity. But Margaret lived there for six years and during that time looked after seventy children for longer or shorter periods of time. The constant changing of children in her charge, the getting to know them all in turn, and the emotional frustration involved in not allowing herself to become too attached to children who were not her own and might any day be returning to their real mothers, must have taken a heavy toll of Margaret's nervous system. Eventually, in 1965 she moved up from the cottage to the house and the cottage then became a more or less autonomous home which was often shared by two families, mothers being there with their children and sometimes fathers as well.

Later, after coming up to the house, Margaret became one of the Pilsdon cooks. She shared the kitchen duties with Gillian and myself and one cooking week in three seemed light labour compared with cooking one week and washing the next which Gill and I had been doing for many years. But undertaking the Pilsdon kitchen was no easy task. As I had done before her, Margaret had to learn to bake bread, brown and white, and cakes and biscuits of all kinds. She had to learn to make jam, marmalade, and chutney, to pickle and to bottle, and every day to cook soups, stews, vegetables and puddings for thirty, and all this Margaret learnt patiently and carefully, compiling her own cookery book with all the favourite Pilsdon recipes and the tips and bits of culinary strategy known to the cooks alone. And Margaret also became the custodian of the greenhouse in 1973. She loved growing tomatoes and they must have known it because, both in quantity and quality, our tomatoes were the envy of all who saw them and the delight of all who tasted them.

Of all of us I think Margaret was the kindest and most considerate to strangers and especially to the shy retiring visitors who often felt so lost when they first came to Pilsdon. Many of us expected them to join in straight away and we were slightly irritated if they withdrew from contact with what must have seemed to them a boisterous, insensitive, extrovert, typically community in-turned group. But Margaret was never like this. Knowing how easily she could herself be shy and hurt and withdrawn, and having a strong intuitive sense, she was gentle and seldom passed any harsh judgements. She always sensed the distress of the frightened strangers and quietly and unobtrusively tried to put them at their ease. She would talk and listen to men and women whom other people had dismissed as dull and boring. This is a very rare gift and I should like to pay tribute here to Margaret's unfailing courtesy to the defenceless and to the little grey people whom nobody else had noticed.

Uncle shared with us all the hardness and privations of the early years. He was my real uncle although known as 'Uncle' to everyone who came to the house. When Pilsdon began he was a widower living in a bungalow in North Wales, doing a little market gardening but becoming worried by his inability to deal single-handed with the size of his garden and beginning to have triffid nightmares about the plants creeping over the hill on which his bungalow stood. So in 1959 he sold the house and came down south to live with us at Pilsdon.

Perhaps the shock and emotional trauma of leaving his home was too much for his system but, whatever the cause, two months after arriving to join us he was in a small sanatorium at Bridport with tuberculosis. He was not new to its ravaging effects. He had been a prisoner of war in a German camp in 1917-1918 and after the end of the war had spent two years in sanatoriums first in Wales and then in Switzerland, after which his father built him a bungalow on top of a hill near Abergele in Denbighshire, and he became the manager of a local stone quarry. But he had wanted to be an engineer and would have finished training for it had not his doctor advised him strongly against such a career. However, he loved tinkering, built his own electric light plant at his house on the hill and spent hours flat on his back underneath his little Austin-seven. He was looked after devotedly by his wife, Lilian, whom he had met during the war when she was nursing in a French hospital for which service she received an award from the French government, and there were no recurrences of his illness until he came to live with us several years after her death.

Uncle was one of the last patients to be nursed in that hospital in North Allington, Bridport. When tuberculosis ceased to be the killer disease it had once been, like so many other sanatoriums all over the country, it was turned over to other uses. And Uncle's illness was relatively short-lived. After a stay of about three months he was back with us ready to take over the care of the generator which he kept in such sparklingly healthy condition that it must have been the best kept engine for miles around. But I do not think he ever felt quite at home in England although his first, and second, wives were both English and although he had spent much of his boyhood in Sheffield. The country-loving North Wales Welsh do not transplant too easily and I do not think community life was ever entirely to his liking — it broke through his idiosyncrasies at inconvenient places. But his presence at Pilsdon contributed a great deal to the feeling of family warmth and homeliness which Pilsdon gave to everyone who came.

In 1962 he married again. Ethel was his first wife's sister and he brought her to live at Pilsdon having first built a small bungalow adjoining the main house, which came to be known as the annexe. He was fortunate in both his wives. Ethel devoted herself to his welfare and also gave generously of her energies to the total life of the community. She had been the Matron of a police orphanage in Liverpool and was capable and energetic and full of good sound common sense. She was a tiny woman measuring no more than about five feet but I still have a Soldier's Small Book which Uncle had in 1914 and his height is given there as five foot three.

Ethel was warmly cheerful and had a ready twinkle. When Danny happened to be staying with us they would play cribbage in the evening after supper in front of the common room fire and her bantering laughter livened the quiet room. But leukaemia claimed her as its victim in 1967. She was only ill for a short time and died quietly and with as little fuss as she had lived. She was cremated in Exeter crematorium and her ashes were sprinkled under the cherry tree just outside their little house.

In 1975 Uncle also died. He had been very lonely without Ethel and often thought he saw her around the annexe. His first wife, Lilian, seemed to join them sometimes and when I went to call him for supper he would turn and say to me, "Have you seen Lil and Ethel? Have they gone through?' or, "I'm just waiting for Lil and Ethel. They won't be long." Gradually senility began to set in and it became increasingly difficult to look after him, but he contracted pneumonia and this hastened the end. He died in the early hours of Monday morning, on his birthday, the 26th of August, and Gino was beside him. Gino was a wayfarer who was staying at Pilsdon at the time and working in the kitchen and he had helped me with all the nursing of Uncle often carrying him from his bed to the sitting-room in the morning and back again at night. He had begged to be allowed to sit up with him that particular night saying he would call us if Uncle grew worse. But there was no time even for this. He told me afterwards that, just before the end, Uncle suddenly sat up in bed and beckoned to someone as though an invisible presence was coming to meet him from the other side, and then he lay back and was gone. Gino himself was deeply moved by this experience and we often talked about Uncle afterwards. Whatever the outward circumstances of Gino's life may or may not have been, he was a true friend and I shall never forget his kindness both to Uncle and to me.

Evelyn was the next to join us. She had been headmistress of the village school at Chideock, on the coast road between Bridport and Charmouth and only a few miles away from Pilsdon. But her leanings were towards the religious life and when she heard of the founding of Pilsdon she felt that in a community such as this she might find the answer to her need for a life of ordered prayer which was still not cut off from the activities and interests of ordinary life. So in 1960 she moved to Pilsdon, a room was given to her at the cottage and she became the sacristan of the church and one of the community chauffeurs. Later she was in charge of the flower garden and flowers were always one of her chief delights. She grew them beautifully, arranged them beautifully and, in later years, made beautiful pictures out of flowers from the garden which she had dried and pressed. At all the big festivals the church was radiant with flowers and foliage which Evelyn arranged with a care which left nothing to chance. She also kept all the church linen in a state of the most scrupulous cleanliness, an attribute which terrified all the unfortunate substitutes who had to do it in her absence. And she also did beautiful embroidery for the church until her hands, roughened by so much outdoor work, refused to obey her exacting demands. All this Evely did with an intensity of devotion which spared her nothing. Everything that was in her strained towards a perfection which, whatever the appreciation of others, she never felt she had reached.

Always Evelyn helped whenever and wherever she was needed. When I was still slicing Seville oranges at 10.30 in the evening it was always Evelyn who came along to lend a helping hand and see that I was finished by bedtime. She loved to share in everything that was happening and I think it was a great sadness to her that, as she grew older, she found it more and more difficult to understand and therefore fully to participate in the interests and occupations of the younger people who stayed at the house. In her heart she yearned to belong fully to every aspect of the life of Pilsdon and the warmth and eagerness of her devotion to it was felt by all of us even though she hardly ever expressed it in words and was herself hardly conscious of its effect. She preferred to show her love for it in practical ways, in acts of unselfish kindness and also in a steadiness and sincerity of prayer which, again, was mostly a secret between herself and God.

Evelyn felt that her innate reserve prevented her from going out towards people and giving to them as much as other people seemed able to do but she underestimated herself. She was much loved and this was in part a reflection of the deep love in her which she felt herself unable to express. So, in her sensitivity, she was often hurt, but she also experienced the joy and fulfilment that come from complete commitment.

And so to Anne who, in the twenty years of which I am writing, was the last of the long-term community members to join. She was no stranger to community life. After leaving school she had taken an art training with special reference to calligraphy but had left college to join the Convent of the Epiphany, an Anglican religious order in Cornwall. Subsequently she was put in charge of their old people's home and then later made, much against her will, Mother Superior of the whole convent. She was a nun for twenty-five years but, gradually becoming disillusioned with the conventual framework, she found, on her visits to Pilsdon, a community style living which was younger and more vital so she leapt over the wall and came to join us as a community member in 1965 and when she came Pilsdon's survival kit increased enormously. She very soon became our secretary and treasurer and in both spheres was quietly efficient, managing, as treasurer, the almost impossible task of combining economy with a ready generosity which gave us both financial security and freedom. She worked quietly and quickly in her little room at the top of the house and sometimes her typewriter would be going from early morning till late at night. She was personally generous too and one of her greatest joys was giving lavish and wonderful presents to all her friends and relatives.

As a nun Anne had driven a fast car and rather enjoyed this image. She loved driving and willingly shouldered much of the Pilsdon chauffering. She also loved clothes and found herself in charge of the Pilsdon stock of second-hand clothing which came to be known as Anne's Boutique and from which many men emerged better dressed than they had ever been in their lives before. She had a genius for this.

But Anne's real gift to Pilsdon was her infectious vitality, a vitality that survived regular crushing bouts of terrible migraine though subsequently these attacks were almost completely overcome by strict adherence to a very special diet. However, when she was not lying flat on her back with the curtains drawn against the light, she was bursting with energy. In the summer she took parties to the beach and swam every day; she organized fishing trips from Lyme Regis and fished with the best of them; and if there had been skiing and skating in the winter Anne would have done both. She was an unlikely candidate for nunship. With all her enthusiasm and optimistic vigour it is difficult to imagine that she ever conformed to the hands-folded, eyes-bent-on-the-ground quietism of a monastic corridor and, when first released from this ascetic discipline, she spent more money on clothes in a month than most of us did in a year. Eye make-up was tried and, one evening at supper, playfully tweaking her hair, I removed my hand as though scalded when her scalp moved under my fingers. She had bought herself a wig!

But it was not all playfulness and fun. Anne came to be in considerable demand as a public speaker. Her experiences as a nun, as the head of an old people's home, as a Mother Superior, as a trained calligrapher and as a member of Pilsdon gave her a wide range of topics to choose from, and she made good use of them. Also she had a quick and real compassion for people's troubles especially those of the sick or elderly and a sensitivity to their needs which never ceased to amaze me. If anyone was ill in bed and Anne prepared the tray it would have flowers on it and thinly sliced bread and a pretty tray cloth and the most attractive china she could find, and when I came back late from a concert or party there was always a hot-water bottle in my bed and my nightdress thoughtfully wrapped round it. Small touches, yes, but indicative of a great talent for caring. She had a warmth and generosity of heart which lighted on us all.

Gillian's strength, Sidney's courage, Margaret's gentleness, the family feel that Uncle and Auntie gave, Evelyn's devotion, Anne's vitality, all these qualities and many more gave Pilsdon an operational base which could not lightly be destroyed.

But if I have touched all the community members with the wand of kindness I must now add that no story of community life would be either honest or complete without mention of its personality conflicts and tensions. Much of the strength or weakness of any community depends on how these are resolved. And at Pilsdon we had no shortage of them. Sometimes two community members would not be on speaking terms for weeks on end and it was not large political or religious issues which divided us but smaller and meaner things, the day to day scuffle over power, rights, privacies, property, economy, and hours and methods of work. In the early days when we were trying so desperately to help everyone we were especially prone to these rivalries and jealousies. Our nerves were strained, our bodies tired and our emotions racked: quick retorts and hasty reactions were inevitable. I was not the only one who, in the early days especially, often cried myself to sleep.

Very few of us had any natural affinity with one another. In most circumstances of life we would not have chosen to live together. We were not a group of friends who had selected each other's company and decided to live as a community. And perhaps it was better that way. We were more prepared for effort. If friends decide to join forces and co-exist and then find huge personality conflicts the temptation is to feel that living together was all a big mistake and that they had better split up again. But if the members of the community are initially strangers there is no expectation and no great disappointment if things go wrong with the relationships. It is easier to try if there has never been a time when trying was unnecessary.

Most of us had to try quite hard to live together. Women in particular do not find it easy to share a house and a kitchen. At first Gillian and I had some battles royal. She seemed to be all the things I was not — knowledgeable about everything domestic, observant, thrifty, sensible, practical, whereas I am, or was then, a bit vague and dreamy, unpunctual, undomesticated, but stubborn and sensitive to even the slightest criticism or discouragement. However, Pilsdon changed me. I learnt the domestic arts, gained self-confidence, lost much of my absent-mindedness and, miraculously, managed eventually to be punctual with at least eighty per cent of the meals.

So, in spite of wide differences of temperament, we all lived and worked together for nearly twenty years. There was something about Pilsdon which held us all. Part of this stemmed from Percy himself. He was a strong leader and had, to an unusual degree, the ability to inspire and sustain people's loyalty. But that was not the whole story.

Many communities, especially the traditional ones, but also many of the modern ones as well are held together by sharing, in essence, the same beliefs, but we were not held together by this. Percy was an Anglican clergyman and Pilsdon was ostensibly an Anglican religious community but there was amongst us a wide variety of belief and non-belief. There were nonconformists, humanitarians, new age visionaries, ecologists, and kindly agnostics. We shared no one religious or political creed. But Pilsdon did represent for all of us an ideal. And there were the people.

Never in our lives had any of us met such a diversity, such a fascinating variety of background and experience. It was a bit like watching 'Porridge' and 'Coronation Street, and 'To the Manor Born' and 'Z-Cars' and 'Steptoe and Son' and several more all rolled into one and then living in the mixture. We never knew what would happen next. We never knew who was going to turn up at the door and we never knew when someone might be saying goodbye. And the mixture inside people was so astonishing too. One man was sober as a judge (are judges always sober?) but mean and selfish while another man was a drunkard but generous and warm of heart. One man was a pillar of the church but a coward while another man had a long prison record but was brave as a lion. We all seemed so alike in our diversity, all speckled good and bad, shot through with every kind of strength and weakness. And yet there was so much individuality, so much that was unique about each one. Every time anyone came or left, Pilsdon changed a little. Each person made a distinctive mark. There were no duplicates.

So perhaps it was this, more than any other single thing, which made us swallow our pride, conceal our fears, battle with our jealousies and resentments — and stay together.

## XIII

Like all communities Pilsdon came also to have many outside friends. One of my earliest and most beautiful memories of it is seeing John Williams sitting beside the big log fire in the common room cradling his guitar and playing Variations on a theme of Mozart by Fernando Sor. He was then at the very start of his public career and was visiting us as a friend. But his serious concentration as he played, the soft notes rising and falling, and the leaping flames of fire, made magic in the quiet room.

And Father Borelli was an inspiration to us all. He came to Pilsdon soon after it had started and sat with us in the common room and talked about his life and work among the children of Naples — the Children of the Sun of Morris West's book. He spoke quietly and unassumingly without emphatic tone or gesture but his presence was its own inspiration. Outside, he laughingly opened a new path which we had made from the milking parlour to the field and which we subsequently called the Borelli Way.

And we were often visited by men and women from other communities. Two extremely picturesque ones in the early days of Pilsdon were orthodox priests from a community in Essex. They wore Makarios-like black robes and tall black hats and only one of them, who was Swiss, spoke any English. So we bowed and smiled, and shook hands, and bowed and smiled again. The other priest was Russian and he was small and old and looked gentle, wise and benign. But, quite unintentionally, we must have given him a nasty shock. A friend of mine was staying with us at the time and, having been given (not by any means *de rigueur* at Pilsdon) a bedroom of her own, had gone upstairs and done some of her unpacking. However, a domestic mistake was made and the ascetic-looking Russian priest was taken up to the same room where he found a pink nightdress laid out on the bed and various articles of female toiletry occupying the table top. Horrified, the old man waited in silent agitation until the younger priest arrived to ascertain that his friend was happily settling in. Finding him transfixed with fear he hastily descended to explain the situation and ask what could be done to put matters right, whereupon Cherry went up with him and surreptitiously removed the offending articles while both priests stood at the window with their backs turned. But next time we saw the little priest he was still smiling and bowing and seemed none the worse for his encounter with what must have seemed like one of the devil's more unpleasant jokes.

It was not only people with problems who found their way to us. Men and women came to experience the feel of community living; they came because their friends or relatives were living at Pilsdon; they came because they wanted a working holiday, because they wanted to flex their muscles after prolonged mental activity; they came because they wanted a retreat for quiet thought and meditation; they came because they were foreigners touring Britain; they came because they were studying community life or wanting to start up a community themselves; and they came just because they happened to find themselves at our door. And in addition to those who came to stay were countless more who came for a few hours to see the community at work, who shared a meal with us and were shown round and made to feel as welcome as sometimes tired bodies and jangled nerves would allow. In the summer months we were especially sought after and every week from the beginning of May to the end of September a large party of people, taking their annual outing, would be entertained in the afternoon or evening, shown all the activities of the house and gardens and fed on home-made cakes and biscuits.

It must be confessed that these visitors were not invariably welcome. Many came unannounced and some behaved as though they had arrived at a Stately Home and had every right to be given tea in the garden and shown around. Sometimes we could afford to laugh at these incidents but rudeness and insensitivity are never really funny. One old lady (perhaps she was short-sighted) rounded on Sidney who is spastic and, in the middle of a crowded common room, berated him for being drunk. Sidney shrugged it off but it was not everyone who could have done so. Sometimes, our guests especially, whose nerves were held in a very tenuous balance and whose self-respect was thin, were left raw and quivering after such encounters. Fortunately the really bad ones were rare but we were constantly on our guard, closing our ranks against the enemy and trying to turn it into a shared joke.

But most of our visitors were genuinely interested in what we were doing at Pilsdon and, if we were sometimes impolite and brusque with them, it was not their fault but just that community life can be very hard and demanding and we were often too tired to be able to make ourselves pleasant. However, most of them sensed this and forgave us our occasional irritability. And we were grateful to them for many things, not only for gifts of food and furnishings and clothing but also for their constant support and encouragement and for the contact they gave us with the outside world.

This contact is something that is very necessary if you live in community. Life can become narrow and smug and ego-(or rather nos-) centric. It is easy to lose perspective: trivial things loom large and it can too readily be forgotten that there are more important things in life than whether $A$ put the hammer back in the right place or whether $B$ asked $C$ before borrowing it. So, like the minstrels of old, these visitors brought us tales of the outside world and information about everything under the sun, and kept us from the dangers of being exclusively inward-looking and self-concerned. They were our safety-valve.

Television too is, in its own way, a method of keeping in touch with events and people. We all watched from time to time and some people were glued to the sets every evening. But it did provide us not only with entertainment but also with this sense of perspective and with a talking point among ourselves. Sometimes, too, when a new guest arrived at Pilsdon and we knew very little about him it could be tactless and unnerving to ask the usual questions such as, "Where are you from?" If the reply was "Pentonville" it could be embarrassing for both the questioner and the questioned. But, "Did you see that programme about badgers?" was always safe and might even draw out a shy, retiring naturalist.

We did have a fairly extensive association with our neighbours. Our cars must have known their own way to Bridport, Axminster, Beaminster, and Crewkerne. We were in one or other of these towns nearly every day on foraging expeditions for paint and wood and glass and cement, to the large Cash and Carry in Crewkerne, to the doctor or dentist in Beaminster or Bridport, and, as we lived in such a remote corner of West Dorset, to the main railway line stations at Axminster and Crewkerne. Many of the contacts made in this way were casual enough but because of their frequency they did constitute a feeling we were not quite living on an island all by ourselves but were a genuine if seemingly eccentric part of so-called normal society.

Percy himself maintained a close connection with the outside world. He was in constant demand as a public speaker and frequently travelled long distances to speak to groups of welfare workers, university students, sixth formers, and clergy, and also to preach, take retreats, and speak at conferences. And this also meant that people whom he had met on these occasions in their turn visited Pilsdon and there was a constant coming and going of passing strangers. This activity was also a big part of Pilsdon's survival kit as the community became widely known and donations, although never solicited, came pouring in. It also meant that, as more and more welfare workers came to know of the existence of the community applications for admittance kept escalating and it was a sadness to us that we could do so little when the need was patently so great.

Many of our closest friends outside Pilsdon were men and women who had originally spent some time at Pilsdon and then on leaving, had chosen to find work and settle near us. Still not quite sure of themselves and not wanting to sever their close ties with the community life they found jobs in nearby towns and villages and came back and rejoined the family circle on their days off and in holiday time. Here is what one of them says about his experience of living at Pilsdon and of how it helped him to return to the outside world:

> Pilsdon becomes a home. We all bring some difficulty, some pain, and need home in some special sense we haven't found elsewhere. Or there is nowhere else to go. Perhaps we have been inflicting a sense of failure and isolation on ourselves for years, habits it is difficult to undo. At Pilsdon it is difficult to be isolated and nobody is particularly concerned with success or failure. Love and acceptance — yes: it is this that can make Pilsdon such a painful place. Dramatic exits are frequent, but homecomings are also frequent. There are no expectations and there is no therapy — apart from the life we have together. The life is also work — housework, gardening, the animals. But it is a little world and its work becomes human. I began looking after the cows. On bad days I would go and talk to them. They told me a lot about acceptance. Now I make pots for a living and come at the weekend to milk. This is my communion. The ritual has to be properly performed. Gill took it as a matter of course that there was only one way of doing things — every morning the cowshed was scrubbed with soap and hot water. I began potting at Pilsdon and after months woke up to the realization I had already set my hand to a livelihood. A lot of things I needed for my life were there to hand, and something else which enabled me to discover them in myself and in my own time. I could call this security, affection and often just time — unpressured time. From these stray reflections you may gather what I mean by saying the intimacy of this little world makes work human. For me, anyway, difficulties with work and people began to take a different direction began to be interlinked, began to appear as the same problem — with myself. It is difficult to hide from oneself at Pilsdon, there's plenty of gossip flying about. Everybody knows what you are doing, what you are up to. Is this the moment for a dramatic exit? Or a time to stay, painfully? Nobody decides for you — and then aren't you just hiding from the world, and how will you get out? This really is like home.

Many of our most faithful friends too were people who enjoyed the Sunday night services in the tiny Pilsdon church — the strength and penetrating directness of the sermons, the full-bodied communal singing, the unusual musicality of what was virtually a village choir, the refreshing tone of the piano, the beauty of the flowers and of the church itself. I have no way of describing to you what this all felt and looked like but those who experienced it became our devoted friends and have supported Pilsdon through every wind of change. We entertained them every Sunday night after the evening service: they streamed back to the old manor house for supper and happy conviviality. In the summer this would be as many as eighty or ninety people and the great bowls of salad or huge saucepans of soup that the cook provided had to be made of elasticated material. Sometimes, especially when it was my turn in the kitchen, we ran out of food just before the end of the queue but most of our friends were blissfully unaware that we then indulged ourselves in hastily cooked fried eggs.

And these friends in their turn entertained us. They invited us to their homes and gave us splendid meals, invited us to plays and concerts, took us out for rides in their cars although there were snags to this as when one well-intentioned but unimaginative old lady insisted on having the windows open in all weathers and complained bitterly whenever anyone moved that they were upsetting the balance of the car. They also came frequently to Pilsdon and joined in and helped us with everything we did: choir practices, Scottish dancing, pottery, weaving, meditation groups, discussion groups, discussion weekends and Yoga classes. We needed all this as much as they did. In most cases it was totally mutual and had in it no element of patronage.

Phyllis started, like so many others, by coming to church at Pilsdon on Sunday nights and ended by selling her home in Weymouth and coming to live three miles away from the community in the tiny village of Stoke Abbott. Soon she had started coming every Sunday to work in the back-kitchen, endlessly washing and chopping mountains of lettuce. Later she came on other days to help out with the cooking and give each cook in turn a day off. She has a lively mind and a training in theology as well as literature and is also an ardent feminist so that conversation was always stimulating if sometimes heated when Phyllis was around and Percy had found someone whose interest in theology almost outdid his own. For a time she also organized poetry readings and we met in the library every Tuesday evening to read whatever poem appealed to us. And in addition she was always ready to give us the benefit of her splendid hi-fi equipment: she taped all Percy's sermons and our festivals and concerts and gave musical evenings in her lovely old thatched cottage, not the least part of the attraction of these being a liberal supply of coffee and chocolate biscuits — the ration of these at Pilsdon was relatively small. It was pleasant relaxing in someone's own home away from all the bells and routines of community life and expeditions such as this were, for some of us, a necessary safety valve from some of the tensions and strain of our existence.

Some of these friends, Phyllis herself included, became so deeply involved in the life of the community that they constituted a kind of 'third order' (although we, unlike the Franciscans, had no second order) — people living in the ordinary world but committed to upholding and caring for the community, needing its support and friendship in their own lives, sharing in all its activities, and extending, as far as possible, in their particular spheres, the ideals of the community — the friendship, the acceptance. Here are the words of one of them.

My future began at Pilsdon, which is to say that what I do now and the person I am now has a great deal to do with my encounter with Pilsdon as a place, and Pilsdon as a community. And the things I plan to do in the future, and the person I hope to go on growing into, are based on that Pilsdon experience.

My first visit was in 1960 and thereafter I visited at least once a year for about ten years. On that first visit I was in poor psychological shape, suffering from years of frustration connected with a physical disability and from pent-up feelings I nurtured living with over-protective parents, emotionally inhibited, angry, resentful about my dull routine job, and knotted up by all the things I felt held me irrevocably back from being myself.

Pilsdon saved me from almost all of that — by people's acceptance of me just as I was then with so much resentment burning inside, by the humbling example of the community's way of life, and by providing a space in which to discover myself and grow emotionally. Most of all it gave me a vivid awareness of the spirit of God abroad and at work in the world. It is still, for me, the place where Christianity is most meaningful.

The attractions of the actual place were enormous. The happiest days of my childhood were spent near by. Pilsdon Pen — the hill which rises behind the house — was the place of many enjoyable outings and childhood fun. It seemed so romantic to return from a town base, albeit a changed person, and then, once there, to share with 'all sorts and conditions of men'. Arrogance sloughed off me like a snake shedding its skin. I saw a new dimension to humanity and was humbled — and stimulated — to going out and giving some kind of service myself.

All this probably sounds too good to be true. Where are the snags? Are there no dark areas in my personal encounter? Yes, there are some. I had many doubts about the autocratic set-up, and was aware of resulting undercurrents within the community which was, by no means, just 'one happy family'.

I came to see that a community life — working, praying and caring together — does not resolve the clashes and tensions that occur when people live closely together. Sometimes, so it seemed to me, people were unjustly or harshly treated and that it was usually only the people who were able clearly to ask for help that got it. Many years on I can see misjudgements and mistakes which make the picture more realistic but less rosy.

What Pilsdon has never been, thank God, is a pious, other-worldly place, or a place to escape to, or an oppressively religious place. It is a 'real' place and can deal hard knocks as well as comfort. It has been a deep experience I'm glad I did not miss.

## XIV

It is difficult to write about Percy, not because there is little to say but because he is a complex, many-sided person, and yet some attempt must be made here to give a picture of the man who ran Pilsdon for so many years, a picture which will be, as far as possible, a recognizable portrait of the Percy who was known to all who knew Pilsdon — its founder, its inspiration, and its leader.

Everyone is interested in power and in those who wield it and Percy himself was always fascinated by the lives and mentality of people to whom an undeviating concentration gave mastery whether in the realm of politics, or religion, or sport. He was impatient of the frivolous: if he played a game he played it seriously — and to win. If the game appeared to him trivial, or he could not master it (a rare occurrence) he preferred not to play at all. Even in the early days of our relationship my laughter when I sent a table-tennis ball flying wildly across the room irritated him as much as his intensity exasperated me. The fact that my laughter was in part a nervous reaction made no difference at all. In sport he liked the steely, highly competitive players whose calculated grip on the game belongs to the mind and to the will rather than to the body. Perhaps this was partly because, his own body being relatively slight, in any game this was his strongest asset.

Power was one of Percy's own attributes. Almost unconsciously he dominated every situation and group in which he found himself though this domination was not of the blustering extrovert kind. At the infrequent parties to which he went he could be quiet and shy to the point of self-effacement but the intensity of his eyes betrayed the force which lay within.

Perhaps it was an aspect of this same forcefulness which led him to fantastic feats of energy and endurance. Ten years after we had gone to live at Pilsdon we started to be able to take regular holidays and Percy's idea of the start of a holiday was to get into the car at 8 p.m. on Sunday after he had finished taking Evensong, drive through the night with only one short twenty-minute stop, and arrive 700 miles away in the Scottish Highlands almost in time for breakfast the following day. And on one memorable occasion when he and Ruth and I were doing the journey together he even got out at the ferry leaving us to drive across in the car and walked the last seven miles after a drive of fourteen hours through the night. Every morning at Pilsdon he got up at 6 a.m., or earlier, to milk the cows by hand (something he learnt to do when we first went there) and the rest of the day might include three hours' digging in the vegetable garden, two hours of counselling, two hours for meditation and reading, a meeting at which he was the guest speaker and always, without fail, a run round the triangle.

This daily jog was Percy's trade mark. Sometimes he was joined by guests staying at the house but nobody persevered with it for long. The triangle, as we called it, consisted of the lanes bounding part of the original Pilsdon estate and was about three miles long. It was a favourite walk with all Pilsdonians but running round it needed more stamina than most people even cared to possess. However, most of the men staying at the house admired, and perhaps secretly envied, Percy for his toughness.

But there was nothing tough about his physical appearance. He was slight in build, not short but small-boned, and he was horrified by the thought, much less the actuality, of those odd bits of flab which most people philosophically come to accept as they grow older. He jogged, dieted, rose early, slept little, and went for long walks in the country whenever he had the opportunity. His tremendous energy was nervous rather than physical: his batteries were highly charged.

Everything Percy did, he did hard, whether it was rotavating the vegetable garden, preparing a sermon, walking, driving the car, or rounding furiously on some unfortunate individual who was strumming a guitar in the recreation room when he was supposed to be planting cabbages. So Pilsdon, communistic in ideal, was highly patriarchal in structure. Percy had very little time for the slow, disorderly ways of democracy: he believed in the strong guiding hand. And for this he was often disliked and feared and there were many who disapproved of his autocratic, sometimes ruthless, methods. But they worked and Pilsdon grew and thrived when other communities were failing through lack of firm, authoritative leadership. Percy was not afraid of being feared, though he preferred to be respected and, as with all of us, a big part of his nature craved to be loved. And he was greatly loved while at the same time being admired, respected, and even feared, by thousands of people who had either benefited from the security and stability of Pilsdon or who had heard him speak at meetings and had come to him for help, advice and counsel.

But there was a completely different, almost opposed, side to his nature. By temperament he was both dreamer and mystic, passionate in his search for spiritual realities, but this side of him was less apparent at Pilsdon except perhaps in the small church on Sunday nights. It was the man of action who was most in evidence. It had to be. Converting a dream into reality takes efficient organization, decisive action, and the ability to shoulder large responsibilities, and if this man of action sometimes appeared impatient and unapproachable there was also in him a great kindness and a ready protectiveness which were felt not only by those near and dear to him but also by nearly everyone who turned to him for help. The 'father' was strong in him and deeply felt perhaps because there was such a close bond between him and the deeply caring but rather stern father of his childhood. It was from his mother that he may have inherited the kindness and gentleness which offset all the more rugged traits of his character.

And Percy made friends easily. People were attracted to him because of his youthful good looks and also for his lively mind. In spite of his keen interest in sport, the hours he spent digging and milking cows, and his quick emotional responses, his was primarily an intellectual nature. It was ideas and things of the mind that aroused and kept his most permanent enthusiasm. And he read omnivorously. In his large circle of friends intellectuals predominated. They were mostly men and women drawn from the various professions, doctors, dons, teachers, clergy, many of them eminent and highly respected in their own spheres, and when they arrived at Pilsdon either for the start of a holiday or just for an afternoon it was sometimes only minutes before they were arrayed in thick socks and wellingtons, armed with a stout stick, and taken for a long country walk during the course of which all their ideas would be taken out for inspection, discussed, and shaken about. They all enjoyed it and came back for more and for this reason there was always an intellectual edge to Pilsdon. Percy liked to think of it as a kind of small college — the sitting-room almost immediately became known as the common room — and there was an open-endedness about this intellectual activity which precluded easy dogmatism.

As time went on Percy found that more and more of his time had to be given to counselling. The community had become widely known through television appearances, newspaper coverage, the diversity of its guests and Percy's own speaking engagements, so that men and women started to come from far and near knowing that he had wide experience in dealing with people's problems. And he was a very good counsellor, never shocked, never judgemental, interested always in what the person had to say, attentive and kind and, above all, never pompous or superior or self-righteous or bigoted. He was always far too conscious of his own shortcomings ever to wear the face of the Pharisee. Sometimes, especially when he was tired as he often was, he could be harsh and short-tempered with the weaknesses and failures of the community, but he was always quick to apologize and to try to understand. His anger often flashed out and some people, when they had been humiliated in public, never quite forgave him but he himself quickly forgot his own anger and wanted to restore the broken relationship. This characteristic softened all his sterner traits, subdued the fanaticism, and made him, in spite of his high-handed autocratic ways deeply loved by both men and women. He had a charm of manner and a genuine kindness which won over all but his most stubborn opponents.

But it was perhaps his preaching which made the deepest impression on all who heard him. Unlike most clergymen he preached directly from his own experience so that the issues with which he dealt were real and vital to the experience of other people. His sermons were never moral discourses, nor were they biblical expositions, nor were they paternal talks to Sunday-school children, but they were intelligent thoughtful probings of important questions both social and individual and there was always the steady reassurance of a God who understands the human heart and is quick to forgive. God was a friend, not a judge, and it was this acceptance of us by God, whatever our sins and failings, that was the corner-stone of all Percy's thinking and was responsible for his firm belief in the importance of acceptance as the basic principle of right human relationships.

The one great stumbling block in his thinking for many people was his undeviating belief in determinism. He had no concept of free will either in large or in small matters: everything was ordained and regulated with no reference to any choice of ours. He believed firmly in the will of God manifesting itself in every circumstance of our lives and, in his own life, when a big decision had to be made, he would wait until everyone's patience was exhausted and even the faithful had grown sceptical, for the will of God to make itself clear. Some people saw in this an occasional excuse for inactivity and indecision and, finally, a justification for whatever step was taken.

He also took an extremely pessimistic view of human nature and of history referring constantly to the near approach of a catastrophic end to all things. Although he read everything from Hammond Innes to St John of the Cross he had little sympathy with the evolutionary optimism of Teilhard de Chardin. This streaked his life with melancholy which was further exacerbated by the inevitable loneliness which accompanies leadership and also by his sadness that our marriage relationship drifted further and further from his ideal.

This ideal was a complete kinship of body, mind and spirit. But at Pilsdon I found my own individuality. I started to experience life for myself, to make my own friends, and I felt gloriously free from the inhibiting image of the parson's wife. I was no longer living, as until then I felt I had been, in Percy's shadow, content to take all my cues from him, leaving much that was inside me unexpressed and undeveloped. Pilsdon gave me, as it did so many others, a self-confidence and a feeling that I had something of my own to contribute. Percy was still deeply interested in theology and metaphysics but I had moved away into a world of people, a world I had never known existed, and these people became for me the focus of my living, my thinking, and my praying. I came to feel that being human was more important than being, in the narrow sense, religious.

Percy was a firm believer in original sin but I came to believe in what I can only call 'original grace'. The reality of the friendhsip and humanity that I found at Pilsdon brought me to a belief in what George Fox called 'that of God in every man' and this illuminated all my thinking. The uniqueness of every single person was a daily miracle for me. Perhaps there are no two pebbles completely alike even amongst the billions of pebbles on a pebble beach, no two blades of grass.

At the same time I was aware of how much we all shared, how much we all had in common. The ex-prisoner ceased to be the ogre-figure of my childhood and became a man with the same fears and feelings as myself and I came to understand the bitterness of being considered 'different', the terrible suffering that tore from Shylock the cry:

"Hath not a Jew eyes? hath not a Jew hands, organs,
dimensions, senses, affections, passions? fed with the
same food, hurt with the same weapons, subject to the
same diseases, healed by the same means, warmed and
cooled by the same winter and summer as a Christian
is? If you prick us do we not bleed? If you tickle
us do we not laugh? If you poison us, do we not die?"

So I ceased to be the 'little wife'. I wanted my share in a wider world. And this was painful for both of us — for Percy because he could not understand what was happening to me and also because he needed my comfort and understanding, and painful for me because he could not accept the new person I was becoming, and although I felt guilty about it I could not refuse to embrace the wider horizons which were opening up before me. However, in spite of these difficulties in our own relationship, we gave of our energies to Pilsdon and the community continued to thrive and to become steadily more established as the years went by.

Pilsdon then, under Percy's leadership, became what is called a success story. He undoubtedly has what is now loosely called charisma. He never asked for money but money came pouring in; he never sought publicity but it came his way in full measure; he made a deep and lasting impression on people even when he was unaware of it and perhaps indeed he never quite learnt the force of this strange gift. It is an indefinable aura which some people have and which brings out in others a total response and it was in the strength of this response that Pilsdon grew.

# Part Three

**Big box, Little box**

## XV

I have tried to give some impression of the experience of living at Pilsdon and, because all communities have much in common, the experience of living in a community, and perhaps the picture glows a little too brightly with remembered happiness and continuing friendship so I must now pause and try to answer a few of the questions which this kind of life tends to elicit.

Community living has undoubtedly become one of the in-things. It is an alternative life-style which is increasingly popular now that the big family — the big box — has mostly disappeared and people live in small-scale situations — the little boxes — in which they are often lonely, bored and frustrated. Communities, or communes as they are sometimes called, have sprung up all over the country — and in many other countries as well. In a directory of Christian communities and groups issued by the Community Resources Centre nearly 400 communities are listed and the details of 88 communities are given in *Alternative Communities* published by The Teachers so that, even allowing for some duplication, the two compilations between them give evidence of well over 400 communities in this country and there are probably some more which have, wittingly or unwittingly, escaped the attention of the compilers.

Now by 'community' I do not necessarily mean a monastery or convent: These are the established, traditional, old-style communities which all have a religious origin, but the modern, new-style community is generally a mixed group of men, women, and children, and the people in them are not all bearded and bizarre in spite of the popular image. They may or may not profess any religious allegiance — perhaps the best known of all modern communities are the kibbutzim in Israel which have a political rather than a religious reference — but whether they are specifically religious or not they do all believe in some philosophy of life which they exist to practise themselves and demonstrate to others either by word or by example. And they do also constitute a protest and a pointer — a protest against some of the inhumanity of modern living and thinking, the devil-take-the-hindmost rat-race of urbanization, and a pointer to the possibility of something less inhuman, less greedy and self-destructive. Many of these modern communities are officially classified as 'caring communities'. They offer some kind of service to society at large, often giving educational, physical or psychiatric help, and it is to this classification that Pilsdon officially belongs. Nevertheless the objections to community life are real and widespread. Partly they are based on ignorance of the actual nature of communities but they are also rooted in something much more deep-seated and fundamental. First, however, let us hear from the council for the defence, the words of two young people who have both opted in the past for community and may do so again.

For me, joining a community was one of those strange 'accidents' in life, but the accident was a happy one. During the three years I spent at Pilsdon I learnt new lessons daily. What I found there was a new sense of reality, that people, madness, death, depression — and even myself — were fundamentally OK. In short, that who you were was fine. What you *could* be then became a possibility, but that was up to you. At Pilsdon I learnt about acceptance. I also learnt about the craziness of what the world calls 'sanity' and about the negativity and 'untogetherness' produced by material values. These lessons were, I believe, never consciously given: it was the *essence* of the community which rubbed off. On leaving Pilsdon I was privileged to spend some time at another community where support and acceptance were also part of the dynamism of growth. Therefore, being 'in the world' came as a shock. From the position of it being OK to be you, it suddenly wasn't OK at all. And what had become a normal way of expressing one's life was simply, in many encounters with people, either bad form or crass naivety.

I can never think of Pilsdon as consisting of people running away from themselves or who are out of touch with reality. It's not possible, I think, to run far from oneself when each and every day someone is mirroring your greed, your hypocrisy, your manipulating and your concern with self-aggrandizement. Pilsdon represents to me something which we were meant to be doing all along. It's like a return to somewhere in our minds we've long forgotten about.

And again:

Life in the outside world to me is much less real — almost unreal because the values, guidelines and goals are different and to me very often seem meaningless. In conventional life what is very often of most importance is career success, financial and material reward, academic and sporting achievement. Here, in community, all these achievements are of much less importance. Here I can just be and try to learn to understand who I really am, and through that understanding try to relate in a more loving way to those around me. If I am not myself, but instead put up defences and barriers, people reflect this to me and there is nowhere to run to. Also I have time to develop any potential talents I may have — and develop them for the sheer fun of it rather than in any competitive way.

Finally I think that the spiritual basis and focus of this community helps to remind me about what's 'real' about life and what is transitory. The only thing I think I sometimes miss is a little more time to spend on my own. But I am happy to forgo this.

The testimony of two young community-minded people. So, what is community living all about? How is it different from any other way of life and why do people either gravitate towards it or sheer away from it with something approaching horror? Is it an escape from reality, or is it an extension into a different kind of reality? In the church community life has, for nearly two thousand years, been a validly accepted alternative to worldly life with all its material values and are the modern communities treading the same path but in more up-to-date guise? However isolated and distinctive they may feel themselves to be are they, in reality, all part of a great wave of protest against the dehumanizing elements in our society?

If this is so it may be part of the reason for the strong prejudice against community life in the minds of many people, especially if their friends or relatives are contemplating it as a way of life. Most people do not take kindly to a protest against their own way of life even if they do not entirely approve of it themselves. But the stated reasons are usually that by opting for community people are evading their proper responsibilities both to themselves and also to society, that they are escaping into something unreal, a fantasy world, and sometimes the feeling against it amounts to an aggressive hostility, especially among parents, because they see no future in it for their offspring, no possibility of 'getting on' in the world or of making any money. Typical parental remarks are, "Why on earth has he gone off to live in a community? He won't get anywhere", or, "It's ridiculous. He's had no experience of the world at all", or, "I can't think why he's done it. It's a useless kind of life." And when people leave a community and apply for a job one of the first questions asked by the potential future employer is, "Why did he live in a community? Is there something wrong with him?"

It is fashionable these days to debunk things, to look for the snags, the contradictions, the weaknesses, the hypocrisies, the self-seeking, and at Pilsdon we had our full share of them: community life is no recipe for perfection. Sometimes, in spite of our profession of helpfulness we were more unkind than people would have been outside a community setting — we were so close to each other all the time, everything was so exposed and the irritations were often almost unbearable. What then are some of the disadvantages of living in a community, and Pilsdon in particular, and what is its strength and its undoubted appeal?

It is true that life in a community for any length of time does tend to lessen individual responsibility, and this was especially true of an autocratic set-up like Pilsdon. Excluding Percy himself there were few areas in which we had to make real decisions, and by 'real' I mean decisions with significant relevance for our own future or the future of those dependent upon us. We were like children safe in the protective arms of our family and cushioned against some of the harshness, and the serious consequences, of life in the world: we did not handle money to any extent, neither did we have to make important decisions about our type or area of employment, nor did we have to face the dilemmas of that employment or, worse still, unemployment.

It could perhaps be argued that this is how life ought to be. Christians certainly have always envisaged the ideal existence in these terms – children living in their Father's kingdom and protected and guided by his strong arm. But for most people this is a Trumpton fantasy, immature, unrealistic, and even undesirable. It is milk for babies instead of the strong wine of life and should be put off with the putting off of all childish things.

In community too you are inclined to lose perspective. Your world tends to become the small one immediately surrounding you and its concerns become of paramount importance while the larger issues of society fade away and grow indistinct. Life too easily becomes parochial and inward-looking and this in its turn makes the petty loom large. Television does help to counteract this a little but it is insidious and thrives in the soil of community living. As in a small village everyone knows everyone else's business and sometimes even more than there is to know.

Another of the snags of community life, and strongly of life at Pilsdon, is the absence of privacy and with this goes the absence of certain areas of personal freedom. Because we chose to live as one large family unit we tended to live in each other's pockets. It was difficult for instance to go out anywhere without explaining your movements. All the cars were communal and every journey had to be accounted for. Also, as we had no private cooking facilities and all meals were communal we never actually chose the food we ate and this was hard on the elderly especially, who tend to need a more specialized diet than younger people. So many of the things we take for granted in an ordinary home were missing from the life at Pilsdon – being able to switch on the electic light at any time of the day or night, entertaining a friend to a quiet lunch, popping over to the pub for a drink, or just being alone in the evening in front of a good fire with a book. Like so many other things about communal living all this could make for the exercise of self-control and restraint, but it could also result in pent-up anger and frustration.

"Don't you sometimes long to be all by yourself?" we were often asked. "I couldn't manage to survive if I couldn't just shut the door sometimes on the world and be all alone."

Yes, we did all long for this and we tended, more and more as the years went by and we all grew older, to retire to our rooms and shut the door.

The lack of privacy also meant that the area of exposure to each other was much greater than in normal life. I have already spoken of the deeper aspect of this and the healing that could come from it. But it had its more superficial side and this could make for extreme irritation. To take a very trivial example: if the man who works in the office with you has the annoying habit of clicking his teeth at intervals you may have to endure it through the day but at 5 o'clock you can close the door on it, and him, until the next morning. But at Pilsdon you might not only have to work with a tooth-clicker all day but you might also find yourself by him at lunch or supper and if you wanted to watch a special television programme in the evening, or sit with your feet up by the fire, you might have to endure his company all evening too. And if he slept in the same room as you . . . . Women seemed particularly susceptible to irritation at close quarters and the women's bedroom was sometimes a seething inferno of rage and resentment. The structure of Pilsdon with its dormitory accommodation, its lack of private quarters even for married people, and its single dining-room, meant maximum exposure of this kind as well as of more serious kinds, and this made personality clashes and conflicts painfully apparent and difficult to heal.

At Pilsdon now I believe this has changed a little and there is greater privacy, especially for married couples, but there is still less privacy in any community setting than in ordinary life if only because you are seen, or not seen, by so many people.

And community also limits a person's allowance of unstructured time even more than is usual if a person is working the regular hours of office, factory, or school. At Pilsdon bells were going all day — a bell to get up, a bell for breakfast, a bell for elevenses and again for prayers, a bell for lunch and a bell for tea, a bell for supper and a last bell of the day for Compline. It was difficult to ignore them even on what was officially a day off. We tended to organize our lives according to their dictates and not according to any personal whims or predilections.

But many of us lived together at Pilsdon for twenty years and some people live in communities all their lives. Also, some of the young men and women who became community members at Pilsdon and then left it have now returned there so what is it about community life that draws some people magnetically and appeals to many more who never join one but look wistfully in from outside? There must be advantages which outweigh the snags and difficulties. There are. Even the disadvantages themselves all have attendant advantages and it just depends on whether you see your glass as half full or half empty.

Although community life lessens the area of individual responsibility, it also decreases the scope for behaving irresponsibly. When people are part of a team to which they have given voluntary allegiance they acquire a sense of loyalty to that team and this considerably reduces irresponsible behaviour and inculcates a feeling for the social group and the knowledge that one's own behaviour has a direct and immediate influence on the welfare of that group. So, in a community, the individual pattern is closely linked to the social: there is an equality of emphasis which is too often missing from social life on a larger scale. People learn in community that 'no man is an island' and this often brings a birth, or rebirth, of social conscience and awareness.

Also, responsibility can itself become, in ordinary life, too heavy a burden resulting, because of inevitable failure to live up to its demands, in a strong and permanent feeling of guilt or even despair, and the absence of this pressure gives a sense of freedom and an enjoyment both of work and of relationships. And even the highly structured timetable is helpful to many people who do not find it easy to structure their own time and reduces boredom with its consequent feeling of futility.

And the absence of privacy too has, as its corollary, the knowledge of being noticed and cared about. It would be impossible in a community for a person not to be discovered for several days after suffering a severe stroke or falling downstairs. We were all hurt and upset at Pilsdon if we were not missed at meal-times. I remember one man being highly incensed because he found himself locked in the bathroom at supper-time and none of us noticed his absence until the meal was nearly over, and it was not only his stomach that felt the pain. There is no danger of being ill in solitary misery or of growing old with no one to care for you. It is still possible in community to be shut into one's own private hell of loneliness but community life does offer a way out which is not always possible in more private circumstances. Although the exposure is greater, so too is the care.

Even the loss of large-scale perspective is offset by living in the midst of a group of people of different ages and from widely differing backgrounds so that even if the eyes are turned inwards towards the group they see more, and at first hand, than is sometimes seen by people living in a more extended environment. And it is this opportunity to meet and mix with such a wide spectrum of character and experience that constitutes for many people the interest and indeed the excitement of community life. This was especially true of Pilsdon. Where else, and in what circumstances, could we have counted as our friends men and women off the streets, from the locked wards of mental hospitals, from prison cells, from schools and factories and universities and offices, teachers and tramps, bishops and knife-grinders? And it was this which drew visiting friends back time and time again to share with us the richness of the human tapestry.

A community is not the place for the personally ambitious: it offers little opportunity for a person to shine above his fellows or make a distinct mark or name for himself but it gives plenty of scope for creativity, the acquiring of all kinds of skills, and the expansion both of a person's character and of his perceptions — no small assets in a world where these things, if not positively discouraged, at least do not come high in the list of priorities.

But perhaps the biggest criticism levelled against community life concerns what people call its unreality, its escapism from the hard facts of life and from its demands. And there is no valid answer to this except to pose another question and ask whether the quality of life in the world is so desirable a thing, whether making money and living above, if possible, the Joneses is mature and responsible and takes a serious enough view of living. So many people in the world appear to be playing at being grown-up, but the façade is easily cracked open and the exposed immaturities find men and women in the waiting-rooms of doctors and psychiatrists. What then is gained by the sophistication which passes muster for maturity, and is there not something to be said for a simpler, less pretentious way of living?

It would certainly not be true to say that our life at Pilsdon was wholly lacking in realism. We lived very close to some of the most basic realities of life both physical and emotional. Perhaps it would be truer to posit that community life is romantic rather than unreal and romantic not in the sexual sense but in being idealistic. It does undoubtedly have an appeal for those who do not feel quite at home within the accepted social framework, who do not necessarily want to opt out but are looking for an alternative *within* that framework. They are exploring a different environment in which to fit a different kind of response to life, a pointer to the possibility of something less materialistic, something, in our case, non-competitive and non-commercial.

So community living is always being tried, with a greater or lesser degree of success, and people hope to find in it an answer to some of their ideals, ideals of fellowship, of service to others, of supporting the weak instead of toadying to the strong, of giving rather than grabbing, of a right balance between the spiritual and the material, of a self-supporting economy and a certain freedom from conventional standards. And Pilsdon is one of these experiments, an experiment in a living and healing friendship, an equality, an unconditional acceptance, just one very small experiment among the millions of other experiments of the human spirit. In themselves each experiment seems a small drop in a very large bucket but together they do perhaps add up to something more and contribute a little to man's attempt to stop the slide towards total destruction and bring some measure of brotherhood and peace to his planet.

Do not be hard on the ideal: it points in the right direction even if it never quite gets there.

"For us, there is only the trying. The rest is not our business."

## *Epilogue*

The tale is told — but not finished. Pilsdon is still there. The leadership has changed and so have many of the faces but the spirit is the same. Every morning people wake to the sound of milk frothing into the dairy buckets and every evening the lights dim out slowly, thirty people settle to sleep, and the silence in the old walled garden is almost tangible.

I think there is some power at Pilsdon greater than ourselves. We made so many mistakes: our own personal lives were often so muddled and sometimes even destructive: there was often more doubt than faith in our minds and more hostility than love in our actions. And yet something stronger than ourselves overruled it all, and has gone on doing so. Perhaps it is the tremendous need of people for this 'space' — a little pool of timelessness away from all the pressures of modern life where they can just be themselves, where they can look at themselves, their lives and their problems, where they can relax sufficiently to find the strength to start again. Perhaps Pilsdon does draw on some accumulated force of energy from a forgotten past. Perhaps it is the strength of unceasing prayer being offered up from the tiny chapel inside the house where all of us learnt that 'more things are wrought by prayer than this world dreams of'. Probably it is all these things, and many more, intermingling with and reinforcing each other. But whether people feel this power, or not, whether they like it or not, and whether they believe in it or not, hardly seems to matter. There is this space and in it people wrestle with their own angels or demons and see their faces and learn their names.

Sit for a moment in the Pilsdon garden on a summer evening. The air is laden with the fragrance of roses and of honeysuckle, freshened by the tang of a sea breeze and the scent of new-mown hay. One or two late bees are still gathering a few last drops of honey. An owl flits silently across the churchyard. It is very quiet on the steps of the summerhouse. The colours are slowly fading from the flowers and, for you, time and place have ceased to exist. You are alone and yet not wholly alone. There is silence and yet you are conscious of the palpable forces of nature all around you. Without knowing it you are inescapably aware of even the tiniest insect climbing the tiniest blade of grass. Soon you will again be standing in a rush-hour queue at Charing Cross: machines will be clicking in your ears all day and at night the traffic will be roaring past your home. But now there is a pause in your life: the simplicities of childhood seem closer and ideals not quite such empty dreams. Accept the pause and let it strengthen you. The name of the pause is Pilsdon.

*Postscript*

What began with Percy and Gaynor Smith was passed on through the leadership of Stuart and Judy Affleck over many years and is now being continued by Peter and Mary Barnett. But they would be the first to say that the health of the Community depends not just upon the Wardens but on the many Community Members with whom they have shared the responsibility for the life of the place. They are too many to mention here but they are held in the memories and affections of those whose lives they have touched.

Over the weekend of October 16th 1998 the Community celebrated its 40th Anniversary. It was a meeting of the past and a springboard for the future. Both Stuart Affleck and Percy Smith preached at the services of worship and as Percy said:

"The wonderful thing about Pilsdon is that, despite inevitable changes it remains at heart as it always has been, *only more so*."

---

If you would like to know more about the Community today, please contact the Warden, the Revd Peter Barnett at:

# The Pilsdon Community

Pilsdon Manor
Pilsdon
Bridport
Dorset DT6 5NZ
Tel: 01308 868308
Fax: 01308 868161
Email: pilsdon@btinternet.com

*Reg. Charity No. 261139*